Change Management Excellence

The Art of Excelling in Change Management

Change Management Excellence

The Art of Excelling in Change Management

Book 3 in the five-part series
The Five Pillars of Organizational Excellence

H. James Harrington, Ph.D.

Paton Press LLC
Chico, California

Most Paton Press books are available at quantity discounts when purchased in bulk. For more information, contact:

Paton Press LLC
P.O. Box 44
Chico, CA 95927-0044
Telephone: (530) 342-5480
Fax: (530) 342-5471
E-mail: *books@patonpress.com*
Web: *www.patonpress.com*

Printed in the United States of America

10 09 08 07 06   5 4 3 2 1

ISBN-13: 978-1-932828-10-8
ISBN-10: 1-932828-10-9

Library of Congress Cataloging-in-Publication Data
Harrington, H. J. (H. James)
    Change management excellence: the art of excelling in change management / by H. James Harrington.
        p. cm. — (The five pillars of organizational excellence)
    Includes index.
ISBN 1-932828-10-9
1. Organizational change—Management. I. Title. II. Series: Harrington, H.J. (H. James). Five pillars of organizational excellence; 3.
HD58.8.H36712 2006
658.4'06—dc22
                    2006013074

Notice of Liability

Staff
Publisher: Scott M. Paton
Editor: Karen Bleske
Book design: David Hurst

CONTENTS

CHAPTER III
Phase 2—Defining What the Organization Needs to Do to Change 33

CHAPTER IV
The Organization's Change Management Methodology. 49

CHAPTER V
Reinforcing Desired Behavior 103

ABOUT THE AUTHOR

In the book *Tech Trending* (Capstone, 2001) by Amy Zuckerman, H. James Harrington was referred to as "the quintessential tech trender." The *New York Times* referred to him as having a ". . . knack for synthesis and an open mind about packaging his knowledge and experience in new ways—characteristics that may matter more as prerequisites for new-economy success than technical wizardry . . . "

**H. James Harrington, Ph.D.
CEO, Harrington Institute Inc.**

Present Responsibilities

Harrington now serves as the chief executive officer for the Harrington Institute. He also serves as the chairman of the board for a number of businesses and as the U.S. chairman of Technologies for Project Management at the University of Quebec.

Harrington is recognized as one of the world leaders in applying performance improvement methodologies to business processes.

Previous Experience

In February 2002, Harrington retired as the COO of Systemcorp ALG, a leading supplier of knowledge management and project management software solutions. Prior to this, he served as a principal and one of the leaders in the Process Innovation Group at Ernst & Young. He was with IBM for more than thirty years as a senior engineer and project manager.

Harrington is past chairman of the prestigious International Academy for Quality and past president of the American Society for Quality. He is also an active member of the Global Knowledge Economics Council.

Credentials

The Harrington/Ishikawa Medal, presented yearly by the Asia Pacific Quality Organization, was named after Harrington to recognize his many contributions to the region. In 1997, the Quebec Society for Quality named their quality award "The Harrington/Neron Medal," honoring Harrington for his many contributions to Canada's quality movement. In 2000, the Sri Lanka national quality award was named after him.

Harrington's contributions to performance improvement around the world have brought him many honors and awards, including the Edwards Medal, the Lancaster Medal, ASQ's Distinguished Service Medal, China's Magnolia Award, and many others. He was appointed the honorary advisor to the China Quality Control Association, and he was elected to the Singapore Productivity Hall of Fame in 1990. He has been named lifetime honorary president of the Asia Pacific Quality Organization and honorary director of the Chilean Association of Quality Control.

Harrington has been elected a Fellow of the British Quality Control Organization and the American Society for Quality. He was also elected an honorary member of the quality societies in Taiwan, Argentina, Brazil, Colombia, and Singapore. He is listed in *Who's Who Worldwide* and *Men of Distinction Worldwide*. He has presented hundreds of papers on performance improvement and organizational management structure at local, state, national, and international levels.

Harrington is a prolific author, having published hundreds of technical reports and magazine articles. He has authored twenty-eight books and ten software packages.

OTHER BOOKS BY H. JAMES HARRINGTON

- *The Improvement Process* (McGraw-Hill, 1987, a best-selling business book that year)
- *Poor-Quality Cost* (Marcel-Dekker, 1987)
- *Excellence—The IBM Way* (ASQ Quality Press, 1988)
- *The Quality-Profit Connection* (ASQ Quality Press, 1988)
- *Business Process Improvement* (McGraw-Hill, 1991, the first book about process redesign)
- *The Mouse Story* (Ernst & Young, 1991)
- *Of Tails and Teams* (ASQ Quality Press, 1994)
- *Total Improvement Management* (McGraw-Hill, 1995)
- *High Performance Benchmarking* (McGraw-Hill, 1996)
- *The Complete Benchmarking Implementation Guide* (McGraw-Hill, 1996)
- *ISO 9000 and Beyond* (McGraw-Hill, 1996)
- *The Business Process Improvement Workbook* (McGraw-Hill, 1997)
- *The Creativity Toolkit—Provoking Creativity in Individuals and Organizations* (McGraw-Hill, 1998)
- *Statistical Analysis Simplified—The Easy-to-Understand Guide to SPC and Data Analysis* (McGraw-Hill, 1998)
- *Area Activity Analysis—Aligning Work Activities and Measurements to Enhance Business Performance* (McGraw-Hill, 1998)
- *Reliability Simplified—Going Beyond Quality to Keep Customers for Life* (McGraw-Hill, 1999)
- *ISO 14000 Implementation—Upgrading Your EMS Effectively* (McGraw-Hill, 1999)
- *Performance Improvement Methods—Fighting the War on Waste* (with Kenneth C. Lomax, McGraw-Hill, 1999)
- *Simulation Modeling Methods—An Interactive Guide to Results-Based Decision Making* (McGraw-Hill, 2000)
- *Project Change Management—Applying Change Management to Improvement Projects* (with Daryl R. Conner and Nicholas L. Horney, McGraw-Hill, 2000)
- *E-Business Project Manager* (ASQ Quality Press, 2002)
- *Project Management Excellence: The Art of Excelling in Process Management* (Paton Press, 2006)
- *Change Management Excellence: The Art of Excelling in Change Management* (Paton Press, 2006)
- *Knowledge Management Excellence: The Art of Excelling in Knowledge Management* (Paton Press, 2006)
- *Resource Management Excellence: The Art of Excelling in Resource Management* (Paton Press, 2006)
- *Making Teams Hum* (Paton Press, 2006)

DEDICATION

I dedicate this book to Candy and Bill Rogers,
two loyal friends who always find time to give a helping hand.

ACKNOWLEDGMENTS

I want to acknowledge Candy Rogers, who converted and edited endless hours of dictation into the finished product. I couldn't have done it without her help. To my friends at the American Society for Quality and the International Academy for Quality, I want to thank you for your many contributions to the concepts expressed in this book.

I also want to recognize the contributions made by the team from Harrington Institute Inc. But most of all, I want to recognize the contributions made by my wife, Marguerite. She's always there when I need her.

FOREWORD

I was in Singapore in 1990 and had just entered the lobby of an imposing multistoried building that housed Singapore's prestigious National Productivity Board. A granite carving caught my eye. As I moved closer, I saw it was dedicated to Dr. James Harrington for his contributions to quality and productivity! I knew him. What a pleasant surprise to see him honored.

This experience in Singapore was a happy eye-opener. Jim Harrington already ranked high in my estimation simply because I knew he had served as president of the internationally acclaimed American Society for Quality. Little did I realize that this walking encyclopedia on quality and business had been honored by many organizations around the globe.

Jim makes things happen. Among other things, he's a prolific writer. And his subject matter has the kind of depth that grabs and pulls you in. I used to review books for *Quality Digest* magazine. For the most part, it required a dedicated, forced effort to struggle through some of these new releases. No so for the books authored by James Harrington. These books added fresh, in-depth insights into whatever subject matter he was dealing with. Frankly, this gentleman is juggling so many "irons in the fire" that I don't know how anything gets done, but it does—brilliantly.

There are a lot of books on change. Most deal with change as a stand-alone topic. Jim penetrates to a deeper level and not only talks about change but also expands it into the *management of change*. Then, powerful links are introduced that explain how change management can be most effectively utilized. Change management becomes one of five "pillars." The other pillars are: process management, project management, knowledge management, and resource management.

Finally, let me say that most books upon being placed on a shelf are rarely ever opened again. This book will not suffer such a fate. It will become your reference book of choice when the subject is change management.

—Donald L. Dewar
President, QCI International

PREFACE

"You are part of the change parade. You can be the bandleader or you can be the one who sweeps up the horse droppings after the parade has passed. It is up to you."

—HJH

This series was written for a small group of organizations. It's not for traditionalists, the weak of heart, or for organizations that believe winning a national quality award is their ultimate objective. This series was written for organizations that aren't content with being anything less than the best they can be. It's for organizations that want to stand out from the crowd and that hunger to obtain optimum results in the five Ps:

- *Pride.* Employees are proud of their work and their organization.
- *Performance.* The entire organization operates at high levels of efficiency and effectiveness.
- *Profit.* The organization is profitable, able to pay its employees good salaries, and pay higher-than-average dividends to its investors.
- *Prestige.* The organization is considered an admirable place to work in and is known for it's highly desired products and services.
- *Pleasure.* Employees enjoy coming to work because they're doing something worthwhile in a friendly, supportive environment.

"To compete and win, we must redouble our efforts, not only in the quality of our goods and services, but in the quality of our thinking, in the quality of our response to our customers, in the quality of our decision making, in the quality of everything we do."
—E. S. Woolard
Chairman and CEO, Dupont

Good is no longer good enough. Doing the right thing "right" isn't good enough. Having the highest quality and being the most productive doesn't suffice today. To survive in today's competitive environment, you must excel. To excel, an organization must focus on all parts of itself, optimizing the use and effectiveness of all of its resources. It must also provide "knock their socks off" products and services, and be so innovative and creative that customers say, "I didn't know they could do that!"

After years of working with all types of organizations and using many different approaches to improve performance, I've come to realize that five key elements must be managed for an organization to excel. I call them the "five pillars of organizational excellence." All five must be managed creatively and simultaneously. Top management's job is to keep all these

Figure P.1   **Organizational Excellence**

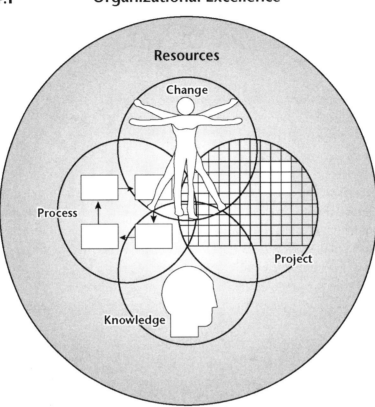

elements moving ahead simultaneously. To concentrate on one or two alone is a surefire formula for failure. Priorities might shift, causing an individual pillar to move from "very important" to simply "important," but it should never shift lower than that.

The processes discussed in this series are designed to permanently change an organization by skillfully managing its five key pillars. None of these management pillars is new by itself, but by combining and managing them together, it's possible to take a holistic approach to improving an organization's performance. (See figure P.1)

The five pillars of organizational excellence are:

- Pillar I: *Process Management Excellence.* We must manage our processes and continuously improve them because they're the way we do business.
- Pillar II: *Project Management Excellence.* We must manage our projects because they're the way we obtain major improvements in our processes.
- Pillar III: *Change Management Excellence.* We must manage the organization so that it can cope with the chaos it will be subjected to by the magnitude and quantity of necessary changes.

■ Pillar IV: *Knowledge Management Excellence.* We must manage the organization's knowledge, its most valuable asset. (Knowledge gives an organization its competitive advantage, as technology can easily be reverse-engineered and transferred to any place in the world almost overnight.)

■ Pillar V: *Resource Management Excellence.* We must manage our resources and assets because they're what drive our business results.

> **"These companies [excellent organizations] implement their results through effectiveness in developing and deploying management capital's intellectual, technical, human information and other resources in integrating a company's hard and soft assets."**
> **—Armand V. Feigenbaum and Donald Feigenbaum**
> **Authors of *The Power of Management Capital*** (McGraw-Hill, 2003)

By effectively managing these five key pillars and leveraging their interdependencies and reactions, an organization can bring about a marvelous self-transformation. It will emerge from its restricting cocoon and float on the winds of success and self-fulfillment.

Organizational excellence is designed to permanently change an organization by focusing on the five pillars of excellence. Learning to manage the pillars together is the key to

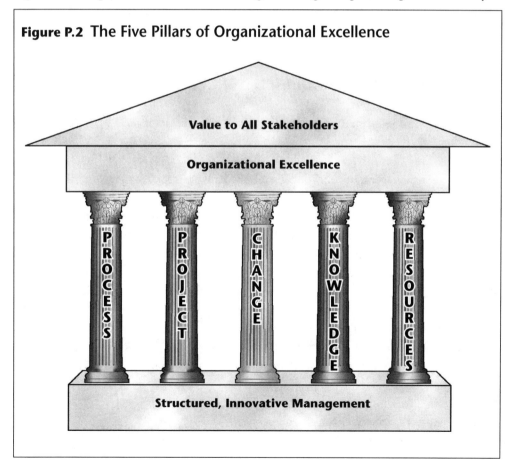

Figure P.2 The Five Pillars of Organizational Excellence

Value to All Stakeholders

Organizational Excellence

PROCESS · PROJECT · CHANGE · KNOWLEDGE · RESOURCES

Structured, Innovative Management

success in the endless pursuit of improved performance. To help you in this endeavor, each volume in this five-book series addresses one of the pillars. The series consists of the following books:

- *Process Management Excellence: The Art of Excelling in Process Management*
- *Project Management Excellence: The Art of Excelling in Project Management*
- *Change Management Excellence: The Art of Excelling in Change Management*
- *Knowledge Management Excellence: The Art of Excelling in Knowledge Management*
- *Resource Management Excellence: The Art of Excelling in Resource Management*

None of the five pillars can individually support organizational excellence. All of them must be present and equally strong to support the weight of success with all of its stakeholders. The challenge that excellent organizations face today is how to nurture an innovative learning culture while maintaining the procedures and structure to ensure optimum performance as well as customer and investor satisfaction. The Five Pillars of Organizational Excellence series was designed to help solve this dilemma.

Because it's important to understand how the five pillars interact with and support each other, a short discussion about each of them follows.

PILLAR I—PROCESS MANAGEMENT EXCELLENCE

"Your processes manage the organization, not your managers."

—HJH

The process management concept certainly isn't new to management professionals; it's the basis of most improvement methodologies.

A *process* is a series of interconnected activities that takes input, adds value to it, and produces output. It's how organizations do their day-to-day routines. Your organization's processes define how it operates.

To manage a process, the following must be defined and agreed upon:

- An output requirement statement between process owners and customers
- An input requirement statement between process owners and suppliers
- A process that can transform suppliers' input into output that meets customers' performance and quality requirements
- Feedback measurement systems between process and customers, and between process and suppliers
- The method by which people are trained to understand the process
- A measurement system within the process

These six key factors should be addressed when designing a process. However, the problem facing most organizations is that many of their support processes were never designed in the first place. They were created in response to a need without understanding what a process is.

> **"Most individuals, teams, and groups within an organization will take the path of least resistance. Inevitably, over time, they will function at the lowest level of acceptability."**
> **—William J. Schwarz**
> **CEO, CEO Alliance and the Center for Inspired Performance**

The Two Approaches to Process Management

There are two basic approaches to managing processes:

- The micro-level approach, which is directed at managing processes within a natural work team or an individual department
- The macro-level approach, which is directed at managing processes that flow across departments and/or functions within the organization

Most of the work that quality professionals do is related to continuously improving processes. Some of the tools they use include design of experiments, process capability studies, root cause analysis, document control, quality circles, suggestions, Six Sigma, Shewhart's cycles, ISO 9000, and just-in-time manufacturing and supplier qualification.

In excellent organizations, management requires each natural work team (i.e., department) to continuously improve the processes it uses.

Refining a process is an ongoing activity. If the refinement process is working as it should, the total process' efficiency and effectiveness should be improving at a rate of 10 to 15 percent a year. In most cases the project team focuses on the major problems that reflect across departments and reap such a harvest within three to twelve months. At that time the project team can be disbanded and the process-refinement activities turned over to the natural work teams involved in

> **"If you [management] create an expectation of continuous product or service improvement, but fail to deliver on that expectation, you will see a build-up of fear and negative forecasting."**
> **—Stephen R. Covey, Ph.D.**
> **Author, *The Seven Habits of Highly Effective People***

Figure P.3 What Different Types of People Have to Say About a Half-Full Glass

- The optimist: It's half full.
- The pessimist: It's half empty.
- The process manager: We have twice the number of glasses as we need.

the process. Area activity analysis methodology, which is discussed later in this book, is the most effective approach to process refinement.

By focusing on its processes and working with its suppliers, IBM reported that, "Between 1997 and 2001, the hardware reliability of our high-end servers improved by more than 200 percent while computing power increased by a factor of four."

PILLAR II—PROJECT MANAGEMENT EXCELLENCE

"How can you compete when more than 70 percent of your improvement efforts are unsuccessful?"

—HJH

According to the Chaos Report compiled by the Standish Group International:

- Only 26 percent of all projects are successful.
- Forty percent of all information technology (IT) projects fail or are canceled.

A *project* is a temporary endeavor undertaken to create a unique product or service.

Projects in most organizations are mission-critical activities, and delivering quality products on time is nonnegotiable. Even with IT projects, things have changed. Benchmark organizations are completing 90 percent of their projects within 10 percent of budget and schedule. Information systems organizations that establish standards for project management, including a project office, cut their major project cost overruns, delays, and cancellations by 50 percent. (Gartner Group, August 2000.)

Process redesign and process reengineering are two of the most important projects that organizations undertake. These types of projects have a failure rate estimated to be as high as 60 percent. The two main causes for these high-cost failures are: poor project management and poor change management. IBM launched eleven reengineering projects that addressed everything from the way the company manages internal information systems to the way it developed products and serves customers. IBM reported, "We have reduced IT spending by 31 percent for a total savings of more than two billion dollars. Since 1993, cycle time for large systems development has been slashed from fifty-six months to sixteen months. For low-end systems, it's seven months—down from two years."

The Professional Project Manager

We liken project management to quality management. Everyone thinks he or she knows what quality is, so organizations assume that anyone can manage quality. This same thought pattern applies to project management, but just as a quality manager is a special type of

Figure P.4   Integrated Management Tools

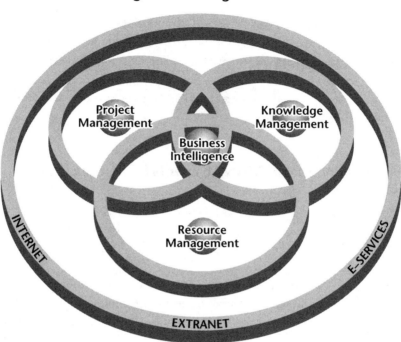

professional with very special skills and training, so is a project manager. Project managers require skill, training, and effective leadership specifically related to project management.

The Project Management Body of Knowledge (PMBOK) defines sixty-nine tools that a project manager must master. Few project managers have mastered all of these tools. In today's complex world, most organizations have numerous projects going on at the same time. Many of them are interlinked and interdependent. Their requirements and schedules are continuously changing, which causes a chain reaction throughout the organization. For this reason, organizations can't afford to manage each project in isolation. They must instead manage their project portfolios, making the appropriate trade-offs of personnel and priorities.

Project Management Excellence: The Art of Excelling in Project Management, book two in this series, focuses on how to use project management tools to effectively manage an organization's projects and integrate them into the total operations. This requires the effective integration of projects, resources, and knowledge to obtain business intelligence.

PILLAR III—CHANGE MANAGEMENT EXCELLENCE

We all like to think of ourselves as change masters, but, in truth, we're change bigots. Everyone in the management team supports change. They want to see others change, but when it comes to the managers themselves changing, they're reluctant to move away from past experiences that have proven successful for them. If an organization is going to change, top management must be the first to do so. This book will discuss change management excellence in detail.

PILLAR IV—KNOWLEDGE MANAGEMENT EXCELLENCE

"When a person dies, a library is lost."
—HJH

Today, more than ever before, knowledge is the key to organizational success. To fulfill this need, the Internet and other information technologies have provided all of us with more information than we can ever consume. Instead of having one or two sources of information, the Internet provides us with hundreds, if not thousands, of inputs, all of which must be researched for that key nugget of information. We're overwhelmed with so much information that we don't have time to absorb it.

"Research confirms that as much as 60 percent of change initiatives and other projects fail as a direct result of a fundamental inability to manage their social implications."
—Gartner Group

To make matters worse, most of an organization's knowledge is still undocumented; it rests in the minds and experiences of its employees. This knowledge disappears from the organization's knowledge base whenever an individual leaves an assignment. In *Knowledge Management Excellence: The Art of Excelling in Knowledge Management,* book four in this series, we define how to establish a knowledge management system (KMS) that will be designed to sort out unneeded and/or false information and capture the "soft" knowledge needed to run an organization.

Because an almost endless amount of information clouds our computers, desks, and minds, a KMS must be designed around the organization's key capabilities and competencies.

What Is Knowledge?

Knowledge is a mixture of experiences, practices, traditions, values, contextual information, expert insight, and a sound intuition that provides an environment and framework for evaluating and incorporating new experiences and information.

There are two types of knowledge: explicit and tacit.

Explicit knowledge is defined as knowledge that's stored in a semistructured medium, such as in documents, e-mail, voicemail, or video media. We like to call this hard or tangible knowledge. It's conveyed from one person to another in a systematic way.

Tacit knowledge is defined as knowledge that's formed around intangible factors embedded in an individual's experience. It's personal, content-specific knowledge that resides in an individual. It's knowledge that an individual gains from experience or skills that he or she develops. It often takes the form of beliefs, values, principles, and morals. It guides the individual's actions. We like to call this soft knowledge. It's embedded in the individual's ideas, insights, values, and judgment. It's only accessible through direct corroboration and communication with the individual who has the knowledge.

Knowledge management is defined as a proactive, systematic process by which value is generated from intellectual or knowledge-based assets and disseminated to the stakeholders. In *Knowledge Management Excellence* we'll discuss the six phases required to implement an effective KMS. These are:

- Phase I—Requirements definition (seven activities)
- Phase II—Infrastructure evaluation (sixteen activities)
- Phase III—Knowledge management system design and development (twelve activities)
- Phase IV—Pilot (fifteen activities)
- Phase V—Deployment (ten activities)
- Phase VI—Continuous improvement (one activity)

"Knowledge takes us from chance to choice."
—HJH

The true measure of success for knowledge management is the number of people who have access to and implement ideas from the knowledge networks. These networks bring state-of-the-art ideas and/or best practices into the workplace. This allows the organization to develop areas of critical mass to implement standards that work, and also provides access to all employees—allowing them to make comments to improve those standards. Even the newest employee can look at the materials and make recommendations based upon personal insight, creativity, and experience.

A big challenge related to implementing a KMS is transforming knowledge held by individuals, including process and behavioral knowledge, into a consistent technological format that can be easily shared with the organization's stakeholders. However, the biggest challenge is changing the organization's culture from a knowledge-hoarding culture to a knowledge-sharing one.

PILLAR V—RESOURCE MANAGEMENT EXCELLENCE

"Even the best ideas need resources to transform them into profit."
—HJH

Nothing can be accomplished without resources. They lie at the heart of everything we do. If we have too few, we fail; if there are too many, there's waste—hindering the organization's competitive ability. Too many organizations limit their definition of resources to people and money. These are important, but they're only a small part of the resources an organization must manage. In *Resource Management Excellence: The Art of Excelling in Resource Management*, book five in this series, we look at all of the resources available to an organization and how to manage them effectively.

When resource management is discussed, it's in the broadest sense—all the resources and assets that are available to the organization. This includes stockholders, management, employees, money, suppliers, inventory, boards of directors, alliance partnerships, real estate, knowledge, customers, patents, investors, goodwill, and brick and mortar. When all of these are considered, it quickly becomes apparent that effective resource management is one of the most critical, complex activities within any organization. Managers and employees must both examine their own performances to be sure they're doing the best they can.

Jack Welch, former CEO of General Electric, has created the following "Six Rules for Self-Examination:"

1. Face reality as it is, not as it was or as you wish it were.
2. Be candid with everyone.
3. Don't manage; lead.
4. Change before you have to.
5. If you don't have a competitive advantage, don't compete.
6. Control your own destiny, or someone else will.

Each resource must be managed in its own special way to assist in building an excellent organization. The big question is, "How do you pull all these different activities and improvement approaches together and prioritize them?" To answer this, we'll present a thorough, total-involvement approach to strategic planning, one that involves everyone— from the chairman of the board to the janitor, from sales to personnel, from development engineering to maintenance. Yes, this is a total-involvement approach to strategic planning; it's both bottom up and top down.

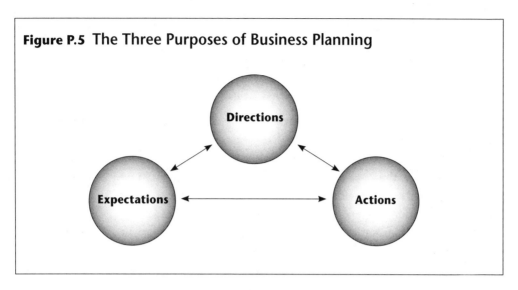

Figure P.5 The Three Purposes of Business Planning

A total strategic planning process (i.e., business plan) has three main objectives. (See figure P.5)

Eleven documents are needed in a comprehensive, strategic business plan:

1. Mission statement
2. Value statements
3. Organization's vision statements
4. Strategic focus
5. Critical success factors
6. Objectives
7. Goals
8. Strategies
9. Tactics
10. Budgets
11. Performance plans

> **"We expect a lot—highly motivated people consciously choosing to do whatever is in their power to assure every customer is satisfied . . . and more. Every day. Without this concentrated effort, attempting a flawless service is really quite futile."**
> **—Fred Smith**
> **Founder and CEO,**
> **Federal Express**

Resource management can't be an afterthought; all executive decisions must be based upon it. It requires a lot of planning, coordination, reporting, and continuous refining to do an excellent job. Too many organizations manage operations by simply throwing more resources into the pot. They may be successful with this approach as long as they have little competition, but even the giants fail if they don't do an outstanding job of resource management.

THE SKY IS NOT THE LIMIT

"You are only limited by what you can envision."
—HJH

We used to say, "The sky's the limit" when we were thinking of the limits of possibility. Today there's no limit—if you can dream it or imagine it, then you can do it, or there's someone out there who can do it for you.

We need to start thinking differently. The word "impossible" should be stricken from our vocabularies. Thinking outside of the box isn't good enough; we must tear down the walls of the box and build a culture without walls.

Our workforce is becoming more mobile. Organizations are cutting back by outsourcing all but their core capabilities and competencies. Business offices are shrinking as increasingly large numbers of people are working from their homes. No organization can afford to pay its employees to do one-of-a-kind jobs when consultants can do them faster, better, and at reduced risk.

WHY DO YOU NEED ORGANIZATIONAL EXCELLENCE?

Times have changed, and our thinking about the way we manage our improvement activities must change with them. Only the very best organizations will attract customers in today's competitive environment. Producing excellent products isn't enough today; we must excel in all parts of our organization. Piecemeal approaches such as TQM, Six Sigma, and customer-relationship management must give way to a holistic view of the organization and its improvement efforts. An organization should wow its customers, not just satisfy them. Customers should rate the total organization as outstanding, not just very good.

Customers remember an organization's name for two reasons and for two reasons only:
- If it produces a poor product or service
- When it produces an exceptional product or service that makes them say, "Wow! That was a great experience."

"We must simply learn to love change as much as we have hated it in the past."
—Tom Peters
Author, *Thriving on Chaos*

If you simply meet your customers' requirements, you don't build customer loyalty. They can be lured away from you if your competition undercuts you by a few cents. Your organization must radiate excellence in everything it does.

For the last fifty years, the quality professional, management professional, and consultant have tried—unsuccessfully—to impose improvement systems on business, government, and academia. Consider the following attempts:

- Quality control—failed
- Total quality control—failed
- Zero defects—failed
- Total quality management—failed
- Process reengineering—failed
- Six Sigma—failing
- ISO 9001:2000—added little real value

The question is, "Why, after great spurts of success, do these sound improvement systems fall into oblivion?" They're much like an old toy that gets put back in the dark corner of the closet when a new toy is found under the Christmas tree.

These exercises in futility stem from applying improvement initiatives to an organization as if they were bandages. What's really needed is fundamental organizational change. Treating symptoms usually doesn't affect a cure; it just prolongs the agony.

These approaches failed because the initiatives were applied as separate activities instead of with the intention of making a total organizational transformation. It's similar to giving a person who has pneumonia an aspirin for his or her headache, thinking it will cure the disease.

From decade to decade, our business focus continually changes:

- 1970s—people
- 1980s—teams
- 1990s—processes
- 2000s—knowledge and adaptability

In keeping with these changes, the approaches to performance improvement have also changed:

- ISO 9001 and ISO 14001—process-driven, lacking in business focus
- Total quality management (TQM)—process-driven, with statistical analysis and teams that are customer-focused
- National quality awards—quality-driven, plus results
- Six Sigma—problem/solution-driven, with a customer focus
- Total improvement management (TIM)—performance-driven/total organization-driven sales, marketing development, personnel, and production. It included organizational change.
- Organizational excellence—performance-driven, including processes, projects, organizational change, information technology, resources, and knowledge management

"Only 5 percent of the organizations in the West truly excel. Their secret is not what they do, but how they do it."

—HJH

The following gives a point score to the effectiveness of these approaches to improve organizational performance.

- Casual—no recognized system (0 points)
- ISO 9001 and ISO 14001—minimum requirements (200 points)
- Six Sigma—problem-focused (400 points)
- TQM—"womb to tomb" quality and teams (500 points)
- National quality awards—result-based (600 points)
- TIM—combined quality, reliability, performance, and results (800 points)
- Organizational excellence—five pillars (1000 points)

"You can win the National Quality Award with 600 points out of a maximum of 1,000 points. That's 60 percent of the way to the goal."

—HJH

You might ask the question, "Where are we today?" A survey conducted by Dow Corning provides us the 2003 status. It included sixty-nine executives from a wide range of industries in the Americas, Europe, and Asia. This survey revealed that TQM was the most important business innovation for these organizations during the last three years. Although Six Sigma has received a lot of press during the past eight years, it didn't rate in the top three most important business innovations. The top three, in descending order, are:

- TQM
- Process engineering
- Supply chain management

The American Society for Quality recently sponsored a survey of 600 executives from manufacturing, service, government, health care, and education. The survey reported that 99 percent of the executives surveyed believe that quality contributed to the bottom line. Also, it indicated that 92 percent of the executives believe that an organizationwide effort to use quality techniques provides a positive return. Figure P.6 gives a breakdown of the most frequently used quality techniques.

"We want to operate far more efficiently. We want to operate at a new level of excellence."
—Robert J. Herbold
Former COO, Microsoft

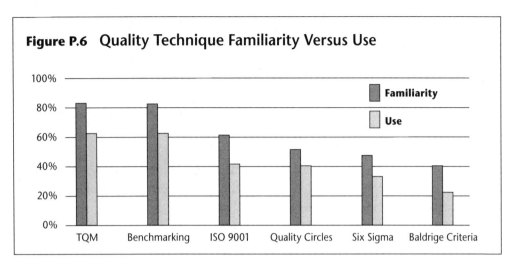

Figure P.6 Quality Technique Familiarity Versus Use

The survey indicates that a wide gap exists between the executives' awareness of quality improvement processes and their implementation. Again, the survey reveals that TQM is used 300 percent more than Six Sigma. The quality profession suffers by constantly changing the name of its activities despite little change in content.

ORGANIZATIONAL EXCELLENCE SUMMARY

"Being good is good. Being the best is great!"
—HJH

When we look at the five pillars that must be managed to achieve excellence, we see common threads that run through all of them:

- Communication
- Teamwork
- Empowerment
- Respect for one another
- Honesty
- Leadership
- Quality
- Fairness
- Technology

"The sizeable gap between usage and awareness leads me to believe that businesses and organizations either don't use quality methodologies to improve their operations or they just don't realize that the processes they have in place are attributable directly to the quality discipline."
—Ken Case
Former president, American Society for Quality

All of these key factors are built into the word "management." They turn an employee into an individual who owns his or her job, thereby bringing satisfaction and dignity to the individual for a job well done.

"The essence of competitiveness is liberated when we make people believe that what they think and do is important—and the get out of the way while they do it."
—Jack Welch
Former CEO, General Electric

In today's worldwide marketplace, customers don't have to settle for second best. Overnight mail brings the best to everyone's doorstep. The Internet allows people to shop internationally, making it easy for them to get the best quality, reliability, and price, no matter who offers it. Customers are concerned about the products they buy, but they're equally or more concerned about dealing with organizations that care, are quick to respond, and that will listen and react to their unique needs. This means that, to succeed in the 21st century, organizations must excel in all parts of their businesses. Your organization must excel at what it does, but its stakeholders must also recognize your efforts as excellent. This will win over today's savvy customers.

CHAPTER I

INTRODUCTION TO
CHANGE MANAGEMENT EXCELLENCE

Change management excellence is the third of five management pillars that make up the organizational excellence methodology. All five pillars must be managed simultaneously for an organization to excel. The other four management pillars are:

■ Process Management Excellence
■ Project Management Excellence
■ Knowledge Management Excellence
■ Resource Management Excellence

(*Note:* Each of these pillars is covered individually in a separate book in this series, *The Five Pillars of Organizational Excellence*.)

> "Handling change is the biggest problem that most organizations face."
> —HJH

INTRODUCTION

> "No person or company should be content to stay where they are, no matter how successful they now seem to be."
> —Stephen R. Covey, Ph.D.
> Author of *The Seven Habits of Highly Effective People*

Change, change, change—we're all for change. We want to see him change, her change, them change. We want to see the organization change. We want to see everyone else change. Yes, we're all for change as long as we don't have to change, but it's a fact of life; we all are changing every day. Our environment is changing, our culture is changing, and the way we work is changing. The outside dynamics, technologies, strategies, and plans are continuously changing. We're left with three options:

■ We can fight it and delay it, but we'll change eventually.
■ We can ignore it and hope it will go away, but it won't, and we'll be overcome by it.
■ We can embrace it, look forward to it, and we'll find our trip through life much more interesting, controllable, and enjoyable.

Definition: Insanity is doing what you've always done and expecting different results.

"People who welcome change make progress.
People who fight change make excuses."

—HJH

As the saying goes, "Three things are for certain: death, taxes, and continuous change." So why fight it? It will happen. All we can do is:

■ Put it off for as long as possible.

■ Change as little as is required.

■ Get out in front and lead the change rather than suffer forced change.

"I can absolutely promise that you will get extinguished if you think that you will not have to change."
—Fred Smith
Founder and CEO,
Federal Express

Price Pritchett's *The Employee Handbook for Organizational Change* (Pritchett & Hull Associates, 1990) states, "It is pretty obvious to people that the stress of a rapidly changing organization can be difficult and unpleasant. What's not so clear to us sometimes is how much trouble we're in for if the organization fails to change."

The history of the world is a history of change, sometimes for better, sometimes for worse, depending upon your viewpoint. But humanity always moves forward.

Civilization has experienced three great revolutions in its history. For the first nearly ten million years, people gathered food in one area. When they depleted the food source, they would move to another area. But then came the first revolution—the agricultural revolution, which began about 8,000 B.C. and lasted until the 17th century. People began to grow their own food, changing from roaming tribes to tillers of the soil. The agricultural revolution forced major changes in the way people lived and worked; humanity moved a major step forward during this period, the agrarian age.

The second revolution—the Industrial Revolution—started in the 1600s and lasted about 300 years. Before this time society had relied on human strength and teams of animals to till the soil, plant seeds, and harvest crops. With the Industrial Revolution, effective use of machinery became more important than manpower. Large factories drew people off the farms, and cities developed around these factories, causing major changes in living, cultural, and social standards. In the early 1900s, 85 percent of the U.S. work force was involved in agriculture, and today, less than 3 percent of the work force is. In the 1960s, one-half of all the workers in the industrialized nations were employed to make things.

The third revolution—the information revolution—started in the 1990s with the explosion of computer and telecommunication technologies. In this revolution, machine power gave way to brainpower and again the way we worked and lived was transformed. In the

1950s, 73 percent of the U.S. workforce worked in production or manufacturing. Today less than 12 percent does (U. S. Bureau of Statistics).

Each of these revolutions required ever-more-complex changes that had to be implemented in shorter periods. Today the information that's available doubles every five years. But these changes have provided us the highest living standard in history and greatly decreased the number of work hours that we have to devote to maintaining that living standard. We're poised for a major breakthrough that will outshine anything we've seen so far, if only we can keep pace with the many changes we must make to take advantage of these opportunities. But our business culture tends to mandate or order specific processes or results, which doesn't work when the goal is to institutionalize a major change.

> **"One hundred years ago, it was the automobile; today, it's access to information via computers and the Internet. Responding to the challenge isn't easy. It requires a real sense of urgency and a bias for action. It requires deep cultural change in an organization. And it requires significant change to an organization's fundamental business operations."**
> **—Joe W. Forehand**
> **CEO, Accenture**

Our new world is moving fast. A person in Munich, Germany, uses his or her American Express card to buy a glass of wine and a piece of onion pie. The card is scanned, the information travels 46,000 miles over phone and computer lines, and the purchase is approved in five seconds.

The ENIAC (electronic numerical integrator and computer) was the first modern computer; built in 1944, it took up more room than a three-bedroom house, weighed more than seventeen full-sized cars, and consumed 140,000 watts of power. It was able to do 5,000 basic arithmetic operations per second. Today's microprocessors, the size of a dime, use less than two watts of power and can execute more than sixty million instructions per second.

> **"When the pace of change outside an organization becomes greater than the pace of change inside the organization, the end is near."**
> **—John R. Walter**
> **Former president, AT&T**

Consider how things have improved since World War II. Our paid vacation days are up more than 60 percent, our workweek has dropped 10 percent, and our life expectancy is ten years longer, just since 1970. We start work three years later and retire five years earlier (U.S. Bureau of Statistics). We've changed, but we need to change even more and even faster if we're to keep the gains we've made. As the war-torn countries rebuild themselves, we have less and less of an edge. In truth, their newer, more modern factories have an advantage over U.S. factories. By lowering tariffs and trade barriers, we've given our competitors access to the world's richest customers. Just to hold our own, we need to change at the speed of light. If you feel comfortable with what you're doing, you're probably out of date.

Why do we have so much change in organizations today? Was it better in the good old days when expectations were constant? In today's environment, organizations have to continuously match and rematch products and services to what their customers will buy. They also have to react to the abrupt changes driven by:

- Technology
- Knowledge management
- Growing population
- Global economy
- Geopolitics
- Culture
- Higher levels of education
- More brainpower
- Increased capability
- Legislation
- Social pressures
- New markets

Since 1991, organizations have spent more money on information technology and communications than is spent on industrial, mining, farm, and construction equipment combined.

We can't complain about change because we're the ones who are driving the change engine. As customers, we demand better, newer, cheaper, smaller, more functional products. To keep up with this customer demand, businesses and individuals must relentlessly innovate, create, upgrade, and improve in everything they do. This drives the continuous change process and the environment we live in. As a result, we live with instability and uncertainty. What excited a customer yesterday doesn't even "meet requirements" today.

"World exports of service and intellectual property are now equal to those of electronics and autos combined, or of the combined exports in food and fuels."
—Alvin and Heidi Toffler
Creating a New Civilization

To add to the accelerating change environment is an ever-growing world population. More than six billion people live in the world today. All of these individuals are trying to make things better for themselves and their loved ones. Every year we add eighty-eight million humans to the earth's population. Every month we add to the earth's population as many people as live in New York City. The earth's population has doubled in the last fifty years. With each birth we gain a new "mind" and the possibility of more new ideas, which will generate more changes. These new "minds" will become better educated than ever before and they will drive the development of more advanced technology faster and further than ever before. This will spur the development of more advanced products, resulting in even more changes.

Consider some of the events that have taken place in the last ten years:

- Fewer than forty million people around the world were connected to the Internet during 1996. By the end of 1997, more than 100 million people were using the Internet (NUA, 1997).

- Traffic on the Internet has been doubling every 100 days (Inktomi Corporation, 1997).
- Cisco Systems closed in 1996 after having booked just over $100 million in sales on the Internet. By the end of 1997, its Internet sales were running at a $3.2 billion annual rate.
- In 1996, Amazon.com, the first Internet bookstore, recorded sales of less than $16 million. In 1997, it sold $148 million in books to Internet customers.
- One of the nation's largest book retailers, Barnes & Noble, launched its own online bookstore in 1997 to compete with Amazon for this rapidly growing online market.

  "Progress might have been all right once, but it has gone on too long."
  —Ogden Nash

- In January 1997, Dell Computer was selling less than $1 million in computers per day on the Internet. The company reported reaching daily sales of $6 million several times during the December 1997 holiday period.
- Today's poorest household has more material goods than the average household had twenty years ago.

The Internet's pace of adoption eclipses all other technologies that preceded it. Radio was in existence thirty-eight years before fifty million people tuned in; TV took thirteen years to reach that benchmark. Sixteen years after the first PC kit was introduced, fifty million people were using one. (James Conford, "New Media as Social Facts: Researching as Shaping the Digital Landscape," 2003.) Once it was opened to the general public, the Internet crossed that line in four years. (U.S. Department of Commerce, 1998.) Internet commerce is growing fastest among businesses. It's used for coordination between the purchasing operations of an organization and its suppliers; the logistics planners in an organization and the transportation companies that warehouse and move its products; the sales organizations and the wholesalers or retailers that sell its products; and the customer service and maintenance operations and the organization's final customers.

"The biggest room in the world is the room to change."

—HJH

Behind all of this upheaval is a logical explanation—Moore's Law. In 1965, Gordon Moore, one of the founders of Intel, predicted that the complexity of the integrated circuit would double every year, a prediction that became known as Moore's Law. After a few years, the interval was changed from a year to eighteen months. With that modification, the prediction has held true. In 1970, you could put about 1,000 transistors on a chip. The first Pentium chips were made in 1993, and had more than a million transistors. Today we can put nearly ten million on a single chip. To help you visualize how big this change is, consider that many of us wear more computing power on our wrists than there was in the whole world before 1961.

"Jim McNerney was brought in as an outsider to run 3M because a significant change was needed there."
—Art Collins
CEO, Medtronic Inc.

This fast pace of change is something dramatically new in human experience, and it represents a major turning point in how our world works. When you double the pace of something every year, you're asking people inside and outside of organizations to handle a violent, continuous stream of turbulence. That's precisely the situation many organizations are in today. Making the changes this pace requires may begin with "technology" but it requires "people" with the capability and capacity to effectively implement the changes demanded. Change is like a hurricane that's blowing harder and harder, reaching more and more people, altering the way we work and think. It's revamping organizations around the world, causing them to:

- Expand rapidly
- Restructure
- Redesign
- Merge
- Revamp
- Downsize
- Enter new markets
- Relocate
- Flatten
- Reengineer
- Align with old competitors

You either tack with the winds of change or you lie still in the water while your customers and best employees go to your competition, and your management team spends its time in the bankruptcy courts.

Keeping in mind the last ten years, just think about what sweeping changes we'll undergo during the next decade. For example, the Standish Group predicts that 75 percent of IT organizations will reform their roles as direct providers of IT services to become resource brokers and facilitators of business-driven demands. Organizational change management (OCM) will help the organization and its people prepare to meet these major challenges.

"We came to realize that important organizational change also has to happen in a company's social structure —in how people understand what is expected of them, in how they are rewarded and managed, in the way that ideas are shared. In order to deliver on our (IBM's) value proposition, we had to change the very nature of work."
—IBM
"We Rewired the Enterprise," annual report 2001

But what happens if we don't change and don't keep up with our customers' requirements? Let's look at one example. In the mid-1990s, Corning was a big success story. It was held up as an example of how to run a quality organization. Its CEO, James R. Houghton, was the example that other CEOs tried to follow. But in the last ten years stock prices have fallen from $133.00 to $1.10. In October 2002 Corning sales fell 50 percent. It laid off 18,000 people in its 40,000-member workforce. Houghton stepped down after 40 years with Corning.

Why is it that so many projects fail? The people on the project team usually have a good understanding of the process and technology that they're working with and they have the knowledge to complete the project. The project fails because what the team doesn't do well is to prepare the people who must change, employees and managers alike, to accept the required changes.

> **"Many agencies fail to transform their process for IT management using the portfolio management process because they don't have change management in place before starting. IT will not solve management problems—reengineering processes will."**
> **—Mark Forman**
> **Associate director for IT and e-government, OMB**

Figure 1.2   **Change Management**

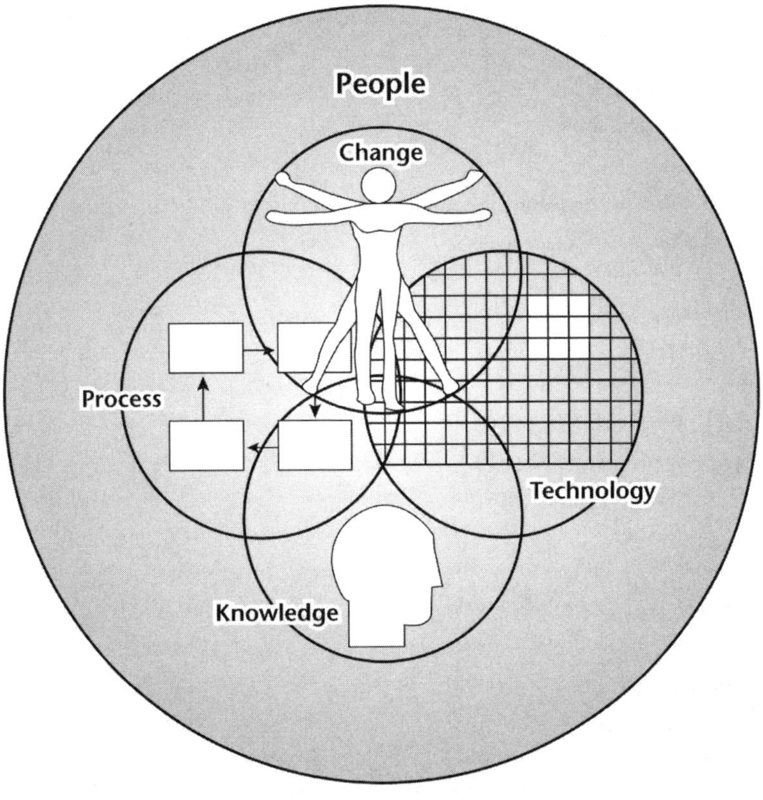

7

WHY CHANGE?

People and/or organizations need to change for many different reasons. Some of them are to:

■ Avoid having their competitors outperform them.
■ Use available technology.
■ Become more market-driven.
■ Increase system flexibility.
■ Reduce costs.
■ Increase return on assets.
■ Increase return on investments.
■ Shorten cycle time.
■ Provide more access to information.
■ Acquire a competitive advantage and/or edge.
■ Simplify processes.
■ Meet new government requirements.
■ Increase productivity.
■ Outsource non-core jobs.
■ Stop market-share erosion.
■ Increase short-term investment versus long-term payout.
■ Increase customer satisfaction.
■ Grow profits.
■ Move the decision-making process closer to the customers.
■ Enter a new market.

Typical Objective of Change

Each change has its own set of objectives. Some of the typical objectives are to:

■ Centralize administrative support.
■ Empower employees.
■ Improve employee morale.
■ Increase market share.
■ Install new technology.
■ Increase compensation.
■ Develop a new business opportunity.
■ Increase span of control.
■ Reduce cycle time.
■ Improve quality.
■ Reduce cost.
■ Establish new roles and responsibilities.

- Streamline processes.
- Become certified to ISO standards.
- Comply with government requirements.
- Reduce bureaucracy.
- Improve communication.
- Transform soft knowledge into hard knowledge.
- Reduce pollution.
- Open new markets.

> **"Unfortunately, many organizations go for buy-in on new processes or systems after they introduced it, and the results can be catastrophic."**
> **—Robert Kriegel**
> Author, *If it Ain't Broke . . .*
> ***Break it!***

THE IMPACT OF NOT MANAGING CHANGE

"The Information Age is over. The Age of Instability is here."

—HJH

What happens when change isn't managed? According to a Gartner Group report:

- Through 2005, 40 percent of global enterprises will wrestle with change initiative portfolios that exceed their capacity for change, resulting in failure rates in excess of 60 percent (0.7 probability).
- Through 2005, 75 percent of enterprises contemplating widespread change will fail to adequately consider their organizational ability and willingness to adapt, ignoring the root cause behind failures of more than 60 percent of initiatives (0.8 probability).
- Through 2005, 65 percent of change leaders will fail to recognize the need for stability forces when subjecting the enterprise to radical transformation, indirectly contributing to undesirable levels of change resistance (0.8 probability).

> **"It's a perfect storm for change in government that we haven't seen in fifty years. There are three forces:**
> 1. **Declining budgets—31 states operate in deficits.**
> 2. **Human capital challenges—50 percent of the government workforce is up for retirement in the next three to five years.**
> 3. **The drive for 24/7 customer service.**
>
> **Government agencies are under pressure to deliver service on citizens' terms, when, how, and where they want it."**
> **—Stephen Rohleder**
> **COO, Accenture**

According to the Gartner Group:

- "Research confirms that as much as 60 percent of change initiatives and other projects fail as a direct result of a fundamental inability to manage their social implications.
- This lack of understanding typically manifests itself in dysfunctional behaviors that, taken to an extreme, cause a downward spiral in organizational vitality and competitiveness—a spiral the organization can't pull out of because it doesn't understand the cause.

■ Enterprises contemplating organizational transformation should first acquire formal change management competencies and develop the organizational discipline to perform cultural due diligence."

Everywhere in the world, organizations generally fall into three categories:

■ *Entropy Organizations.* These organizations strive to maintain the status quo at all costs, even as the organization erodes with time.

■ *Chaos Organizations.* These organizations live in a random, changing environment. They're always in a crisis mode of operation. There's little or no control over what and how the organization is changing.

■ *Controlled Organizations.* These organizations have visions of how they want and need to change. Change is controlled as part of an overall plan. Measurements are in place that allows them to predict outcomes and, if their desired outcomes are in jeopardy, to take action before they become a crisis.

One large automotive manufacturer spent more than $48 billion on robots and other advanced technologies, only to have its profits plummet. The company finally admitted publicly that it had made an error in putting its emphasis on technology rather than people.

In another case, a food company spent millions on computer technologies intended to make it more customer-focused; it was to provide up-to-the-minute information about who was buying which products in which region. The system was well-designed, but the results were an utter failure. The people who were supposed to use the system wouldn't drop their traditional, familiar way of doing business. As a result, the new system was disbanded.

WHAT IS CHANGE?

Human beings are extremely control-oriented. We feel most comfortable when our environment is controlled, stable, predictable, and when our expectations are being met. In fact, the definition of the term status quo is "when expectations are being met." We may not like the environment we're in, but we know it, understand it, and have adjusted to it. Change occurs when this balance shifts and expectations are disrupted. So change can be defined as "a disruption in your expectation."

"Change is shorthand for opportunity, and if you can be a little bit ahead of shifts in business, the opportunities can be big."
—Fred Smith
Founder and CEO,
Federal Express

If you came into your office one morning and your desk and chair were gone, that would disrupt your expectations. Imagine how you would feel. Would the change upset you? Would you yell at your manager or your secretary, "Who took my desk and chair?" Would you stop being productive? Would you fear that you'd been fired and somebody forgot to tell you? All of these things happen in the change environment. When change occurs, stability in the organization falls. The stress level intensifies. Productivity decreases, anxiety runs high, fear infects everyone, and the level of conflict increases among the employees. But you can't say change is "bad medicine" because some people don't like its taste. Remember that change is really an opportunity.

Further, you must realize that with all the changes, people will make errors. There's no way around it. As Art Collins, CEO of Medtronics, put it, "People will make mistakes. You've got to give people the opportunity to make mistakes, to fail, and not be crucified for doing it. Now you don't want them to fail repeatedly, but you've got to encourage them to look at change as an opportunity rather than a risk."

At first glance, the reaction to this situation would seem to be, "Slow down; don't change so fast." Gradual change may seem the safest way to proceed but that's not normally the case. Big changes call for drastic action. You need to hit hard with bold strokes that shatter the status quo. That's how you get people's attention and support.

Philip Crosby's zero defects concept was good in the 1970s, but it flies in the face of managing transition and change. No organization can take the time to ensure its processes for change are perfect. If it did, it would never make any changes. Do what you can to prevent and correct errors, and then take a risk. For example, every time we proofed this book we found improvements we would've liked to make, but at some point we had to stop editing and let it go to the publisher. It's called "time-boxing" your efforts.

MURPHY'S LAW APPLIED TO CHANGE MANAGEMENT

A number of variations on Murphy's Law—anything that can go wrong will go wrong— can be applied directly to organizational change management. Some of them are:

- Nothing is as easy as it looks.
- Everything takes longer than you think.
- Inside every large problem is a series of small problems struggling to get out.
- The other line always moves faster.
- Whatever hits the fan will not be evenly distributed.
- Any tool dropped while repairing a car will roll beneath the exact center.
- The repairman will never have seen a model quite like yours.
- The light at the end of the tunnel is the headlamp of an oncoming train.

"The 'good old days' were last week, and this week
the rules have changed."

—HJH

WANT TO HELP OTHERS CHANGE?
TRY STARTING WITH YOURSELF!

The following is a paraphrased excerpt from Billy Arcement's June 2004 newsletter, *News From the Swamp*:

We've all heard people say (or perhaps you've even said it), I'm going to change my spouse, friend, enemy, or employee. The truth is, you can't change anyone unless they're a willing participant.

Forget changing others. Start working on yourself. Begin thinking differently about the individual. Focus on developing a caring, non-biased, forgiving attitude. Forget past transgressions that may have occurred and concentrate on what you want to happen in the future. Talk to the individual and share your efforts and sincerely ask him or her to undertake a similar mindset about you. Establish a periodic discussion time to share your personal observations regarding where the relationship is moving. Candid exchanges are the only way to make progress. There's power in one-on-one exchanges that broadens the opportunity for success.

> **"The best helping hand I ever got was at the end of my own arm."**
> **—Mark Twain**

If both parties are willing participants, positive change can and will occur. But a most important part is to have everyone let go of the past. You can't saw sawdust so quit rehashing old wounds. The resolution is to behave differently in the future.

> **"Nothing of any great consequence has been accomplished without discipline and a will to change or improve."**
> **—Billy Arcement**
> **Author, *Searching for Success***

There's a bit of a risk here but if you sincerely feel that unless change occurs the relationship is doomed to fail, you really have nothing to risk by trying this approach because failure is eminent without change occurring.

There's within each of us a hidden power that surfaces whenever we need a boost of energy to overcome life's obstacles. It's a four-letter word, but a good one. We call it hope.

Hope is the magic motivator that keeps our dreams alive and our attitude positive. It's the driver of the human spirit, a builder of dreams. But the dark side of hope is often where we plant ourselves. It's called hopelessness. When we succumb to the weight of hopelessness, we give up on our dreams. We discourage all personal initiatives.

The beauty of life is that we're always free to make the choice to turn hopelessness into hope. Each day we can choose to become better, stronger, more productive individuals. What choice will you make—hope or hopelessness?

Change Is Always Personal

Change is a very personal thing. Each individual changes every day, and change affects each individual every day. Our personal situations influence how we view other people, organizations, and countries, but as the environment around us changes, we change with it. At times the environmental changes can turn our thinking 180 degrees. This change may not always be in a positive direction. Figure 1.3 depicts how a woman and a man's perceptions of each other change as they go from courtship, through marriage, to divorce.

Less than 50 percent of the work force is now employed in full-time jobs. Many are working in temporary or part-time jobs, either because they want it that way or because that's all that's available. The really new trend is for people to be self-employed or to do consulting work.

CHANGE IS NOT ALWAYS POSITIVE

Before Marriage	During Marriage	After Divorce
Charming Interesting Witty Temptress	Thoughtful Caring Nurturing Angel	Money-hungry Vindictive Selfish Witch
Interesting Thoughtful Gallant Pursuer	Protective Caring Wise White Knight	Mean Penny-pinching Inconsiderate Devil

"The future belongs to those who believe in the beauty of their dreams."
—Eleanor Roosevelt
Former first lady

THE THREE PHASES OF PERFORMANCE IMPROVEMENT MANAGEMENT METHODOLOGY

Three phases make up the performance improvement management methodology; they're subdivided into nine activities. (See figure 1.4.)

Phase 1—Defining How the Organization Needs to Change: Developing Future-State Visions.

- Activity 1.1—Conduct a present-state assessment.
- Activity 1.2—Develop key business drivers' vision statements.
- Activity 1.3—Develop performance improvement goals.
- Activity 1.4—Define desired behaviors and habit patterns.

"Everybody has accepted by now that change is unavoidable. But that still implies that change is like death and taxes—it should be postponed as long as possible and no change would be vastly preferable. But in a period of upheaval, such as the one we are living in, change in the norm."
—Peter Drucker
Author of *Management Challenges for the 21st Century*

Phase 2—Defining What the Organization Needs to Do to Change

- Activity 2.5—Develop the individual performance improvement management plans.
- Activity 2.6—Combine the individual performance improvement management plans (total performance improvement management plan).
- Activity 2.7—Develop a 90-day action plan.

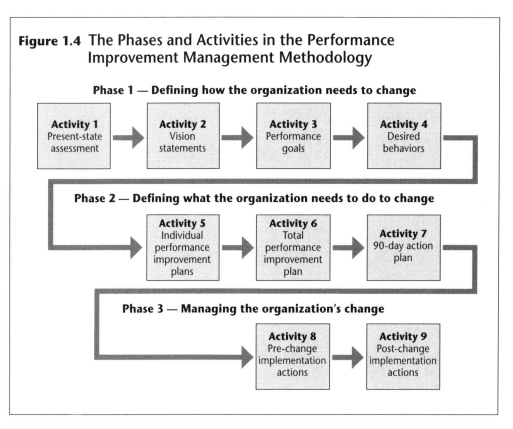

Figure 1.4 The Phases and Activities in the Performance Improvement Management Methodology

Phase 1 — Defining how the organization needs to change

Activity 1
Present-state assessment

Activity 2
Vision statements

Activity 3
Performance goals

Activity 4
Desired behaviors

Phase 2 — Defining what the organization needs to do to change

Activity 5
Individual performance improvement plans

Activity 6
Total performance improvement plan

Activity 7
90-day action plan

Phase 3 — Managing the organization's change

Activity 8
Pre-change implementation actions

Activity 9
Post-change implementation actions

"**It must be considered that there is nothing more difficult to carry out, nor more doubtful of success, nor more dangerous to handle, than to initiate a new order of things.**"
— **Niccolo Machiavelli 16th-century Italian statesman**

Phase 3—Managing the Organization's Change Process

■ Activity 3.8—Execute pre-change implementation actions.

■ Activity 3.9—Execute post-change implementation actions.

CHAPTER II

PHASE 1—DEFINING HOW THE ORGANIZATION NEEDS TO CHANGE

"If you haven't changed your mind in the last month,
you probably are dead."

—HJH

Phase 1 is divided into four activities. They are:
- Activity 1.1—Conduct a present-state assessment.
- Activity 1.2—Develop key business drivers' vision statements.
- Activity 1.3—Develop performance improvement goals.
- Activity 1.4—Define desired behaviors and habit patterns.

ACTIVITY 1.1—CONDUCT A PRESENT-STATE ASSESSMENT

The organization has control over relatively few things. It doesn't control the economy, its customers, its competition, its suppliers, government regulations, the stock market, or the weather. The only thing that the organization can change is the environment within the organization. And so they do, but most organizations take a piecemeal approach to improvement and change. They follow the crowd, doing what everyone else is doing. We're a fad culture. Xerox does benchmarking, so we need to do it too. GE does Six Sigma, so let's do it (whatever it is)! Sprint is outsourcing information technology (IT), so it must

be a good thing for us. Organizations are like a boy in a candy shop who doesn't have to pay for his candy. Everything looks good, so he devours it quickly before the next tempting morsel comes along. The result, of course, is a very sick boy.

Rather than jump at the latest improvement fad, any organization first should determine whether it's a suitable fit. The first step is to assess the present state of the organization. I recommend that an independent group (i.e., a consulting group) conduct the assessment and that the individual pieces of input to the assessment be kept confidential. The consultant should conduct the following assessments to define the present-state status of the organization and where it can improve:

- Customer satisfaction assessment
- Culture assessment
- Improvement needs assessment
- Historical change management assessment
- Business drivers' assessment
- Employee/management opinion survey

> **"Choosing the future is not just a matter of wishing for a better tomorrow. We make our choices through our actions, not our thoughts. Merely dreaming about a better world and community accomplishes nothing. We must translate our dreams into practical decisions we make concerning how we live our lives."**
> **—Edward Cornish**
> **Author, *Futuring: The Exploration of the Future***

These assessments need to reflect input from all levels and types of people in the organization. They can't be supported by surveys alone. One-on-one management interviews and employee-focus groups provide the types of insights that are required.

Customer Satisfaction Assessment

The customer satisfaction assessment starts by reviewing the way the organization collects customer satisfaction data. If the process is good and the data collection forms contain the required data, it won't be necessary to conduct a customer survey, as the data on hand will provide the needed information. The data analysis must be supplemented with direct discussions with typical customers.

Culture Assessment

The culture assessment needs to address both the formal and informal culture of the organization. The formal culture is defined by things such as the organization's vision, mission, principles, values, strategic focus, objectives, goals, and operating procedures. These should be well documented, making it easy to evaluate them. The informal culture is the way people interpret these documents. This means the way people within the organization behave, what they expect, what they believe, and what they assume. The informal culture is the way the organization really operates and it's the one that is most important. It makes little difference what is written down or what the managers say. It's the culture of the organization and the way people react on a day-to-day basis that's most important.

"People listen to what the tongue in management's mouth says, but they believe what the tongue in management's shoe does."

—HJH

In other words, your employees listen to what you say, but they react to what you do. Everyone from the CEO to the floor sweeper should be governed by the same rules of behavior.

The only way to assess the informal culture is by observation, talking to all levels of management and employees, and holding focus-group discussions. A culture assessment will help collect data, but the real culture can be identified only through one-on-one discussions.

Improvement Needs Assessment

The improvement needs assessment is a very important driver of the change management process. Often there are very different improvement needs for different levels of people within all organizations. Things that aren't important to the executive team may be very important to the employees and will make the difference between success or failure. We find that a well-designed survey, which is conducted with five groups of people, works well to satisfy the need. The same survey should be given to:

■ Executives
■ Middle management
■ First-line managers (supervisors)
■ Support employees
■ Production employees

This survey assesses the opportunities for improvement and change and ranks the priorities of each of the five groups. This allows comparison of the five groups' priorities. At least the five highest priorities of all five groups should be included in the change process.

Historical Change Management Assessment

The historical change management assessment is also an important input to the change management process. People's beliefs and behaviors are the result of their experiences. If the organization has tried to make changes in the past and this proved to be a positive experience for the people who were affected by the change, then there will be far less resistance to a new change initiative. However, if your employees have been exposed to unsuccessful changes or to changes that have had a negative impact on them, then they will be much more resistant to new change initiatives.

The successes and failures of the projects that were undertaken in the past have a big influence on how future changes will be accepted or rejected by the staff. If the past change initiatives were unsuccessful, the general attitude will be, "This, too, will pass." It's important that you understand these attitudes and develop plans to offset any negative patterns.

To analyze barriers that will arise from past implementation problems and that must be overcome, we recommend using the past implementation problems assessment survey. Past experience in carrying out change sets the stage for expectations of current and future change. It's important to understand where problems may have occurred in the past so that they can be corrected and so that they are designed out of new plans for carrying out change. An organization's track record of implementing change is one of the clearest indicators of the likelihood of future performance unless it does something different. The interactive tool, implementation problems assessment, identifies common barriers to carrying out change. It allows an organization to benefit from mistakes of the past in addressing the implementation issues of future change projects.

The change history survey can be used to identify risk based upon past experience. This diagnostic tool identifies issues in an organization's history that have been significant barriers to the successful implementation of previous change initiatives. The survey should be completed by a sample of individuals representing important constituencies within the organization. Conducting the survey early in the project allows important concerns to surface about inhibitors that have influenced past change efforts. This enables managers, who are responsible for change projects, to quickly assess implementation barriers and their implications. This information is presented in a report that summarizes the factors that distinguish successful organizations from those that fail when implementing change.

Typical statements that the employees are asked to evaluate on an implementation history assessment are:

- Risk-taking has been discouraged and creative ideas have been ignored because too much emphasis has been placed on finding and correcting errors.
- Making change decisions in this organization has required approval at too many levels.
- Management has a history of not being disciplined enough to get day-to-day tasks done.
- During past change efforts, cooperation and support between work areas (or departments) have been weak or nonexistent.

Each statement is rated on a scale of one to ten. A "one" indicates that the statement is inconsistent with how the organization has implemented changes in the past. A "ten" indicates that the statement is consistent with how the organization has done so. All statements that have an average of seven or above are high-risk barriers to change, and action plans to deal with them must be prepared to offset the organization's past performance. Statements whose average rating is between four and six have a guarded prognosis for successful implementation of new change initiatives and should be considered in preparing the OCM plan.

Each characteristic can range from a very positive enabler to a very negative barrier to the change activity. Mitigation plans should be prepared and put in place for all characteristics that are high-risk barriers and for selected characteristics that aren't enablers.

Normally change history surveys are conducted at a minimum of three levels within the organization.

- Executive level
- Management level
- Employee level

Business Drivers' Assessment

Many things in business are beyond our control. We can't control inflation, our competition, oil prices, the weather, outside technologies, etc. What we must do is define the organization's key business drivers. Most organizations generally have eight to ten key business drivers. Typical business drivers are:

- Measurement drivers
- Leadership and support drivers
- Training drivers
- Customer and/or partnership drivers
- Business processes drivers
- Knowledge management drivers

> **"We cannot direct the wind, but we can adjust the sales."**
> **—Bertha Calloway**
> **Founder, Great Plains**
> **Black Museum**

Definition: Business drivers are things that the organization can control and change that have a major impact upon the way an organization performs.

Once you've defined the key business drivers, you should assess the status of each of these business drivers. An effective tool in helping management define the present state of the organization's business drivers is a business driver maturity grid. Figure 2.1 is a twelve-level maturity grid for management leadership and support.

Each executive will select a phrase on the maturity grid that best describes the as-is status of the organization. The purpose of this analysis is two-fold:

- To provide the executive a view of how the business drivers could evolve.
- To select the statement for each of the key business drivers that best describes how the organization is operating today (the present status or as-is status)

The way the analysis is conducted:

- The analysis is conducted when the executive is alone, without discussion with anyone else. The results are considered personal and confidential and should not be identifiable as coming from a particular individual.

Figure 2.1 Performance Goals Example

BUSINESS DRIVER: MANAGEMENT LEADERSHIP AND SUPPORT

Scale

1. Managers give orders. Employees are responsible for following them exactly without question. Management gets credit for all successes; employees are blamed for failures.

2. Managers give orders. Employees are responsible for following them exactly, but they are allowed to question them. Employees are blamed when they don't follow orders.

3. Managers are responsible for results; workers respond to the directives of management.

4. Managers recognize the need for change. Recognition and rewards begin to be a part of the motivation process. Managers start looking for and praising people who do the right things right.

5. Managers create a vision of the preferred future, which leads to group development of the "mission." An organizationwide plan for achieving the mission has been developed. All managers are trained in participative management techniques. Teams are formed to work on problem solving and improvement opportunities.

6. A continuous improvement process is launched; team building and problem-solving training are provided to everyone. Managers recognize the need to be process-oriented. Progress has been made in building pride of accomplishment and self-esteem. Supervisors and managers are selected based primarily on their leadership ability.

7. Managers begin teaching, coaching, and working with their people on continuous improvement. Managers are treating quality and productivity as one. There are numerous examples of team building. An error-free performance standard is being used.

8. Management is working to change systems/processes that their organization has identified as barriers to achieving the organization's mission. "Management by walking around" is actively practiced. All employees are active members of a team. Supervisors and their teams use employee surveys to improve.

9. Managers tailor their organizations to facilitate continuous improvement. Quality and productivity performance levels and improvement "projects" are routinely reviewed with teams/individuals. All employees' output quality is measured and reported back to them.

10. Managers apply appropriate situational leadership concepts to stimulate groups and individuals in implementing a continuous improvement process. Managers are using statistical thinking. Teams are starting to set work standards. Promotions go to the people who prevent errors. A five-year plan that includes improvement activities is defined and understood by all.

11. Recognition and rewards clearly flow to those who are using a continuous improvement process. Firefighting is left to lower management and employees. Upper and middle management spend much of their time working with employees in their work areas, talking to customers, or doing long-range planning.

12. The culture includes the effective use of a continuous improvement process to constantly improve quality, productivity, and employee morale. Workers are responsible for results; managers are responsive to their needs. Employees understand and support long-term quality goals. Employees are setting their own time standards. The majority of management time is spent preventing errors.

- The executive should read all twelve statements.
- Next, the executive should start over by reading the first statement to see if it applies in its entirety or if the organization has progressed beyond this point. If the organization meets either of these conditions, the executive should go to the next statement and make a similar assessment. He or she should continue until reaching a statement that doesn't apply in its entirety and then record the number of the previous statement, which reflects the maturity level that the organization does comply with.

These surveys should be collected, and a graph for each key business driver be prepared. (See figure 2.2.)

By analyzing these graphs, you can learn a lot about the organization. In the example portrayed in figure 2.2, maturity level four is the highest-rated maturity level and 4.38 is the average of the total population. Statement four reads, "Managers recognize the need for change. Recognition and rewards begin to be part of the motivation process. Managers start looking for and praising people doing the right things right."

The graph shows that, of the thirty-two executives surveyed, their understanding about how the organization was managed varied from a maturity level of one to eleven.

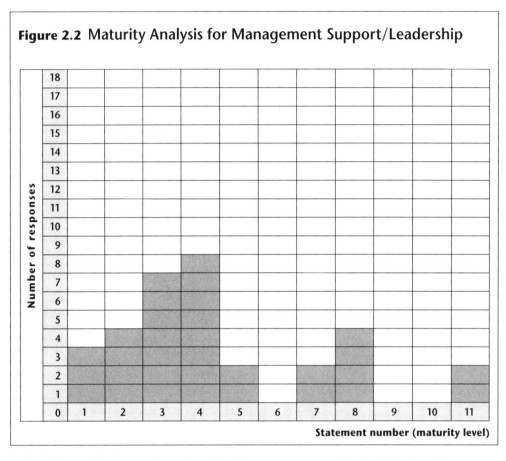

Figure 2.2 Maturity Analysis for Management Support/Leadership

- Level One—Managers give orders. Employees are responsible for following them exactly without question. Managers get credit for all successes; employees are blamed for failures.
- Level Eleven—Recognition and rewards clearly flow to those who are using a continuous improvement process. Firefighting is left to lower management and employees. Upper and middle management spend much of their time working with the employees in their work areas, talking to customers, or doing long-range planning.

This is a range of eleven. A range in excess of three is considered poor; it indicates that the management team doesn't have a common understanding of how the organization functions, without which it will be very difficult to develop a performance improvement plan because the different managers will have very different views on how the organization needs to change. The best that can be hoped for is that they can all agree on how the organization should be functioning.

Now the executive team should meet and review the survey data. During this meeting, they will:

- Discuss why the different executives view the organization in very different ways for those areas where the range is greater than three.
- Modify the average maturity statement to reflect the organization's actual status.
- Develop a set of preliminary vision statements for each of the key business drivers. These vision statements will define how the business drivers should evolve through the next three to five years.

Employee and Management Opinion Survey

An employee and management opinion survey is an effective way of defining problems and opportunities for change. It's a complete assessment of the total operation as viewed by its impact on the individual. It doesn't focus on improving the total performance of the organization. For this reason, it may be put off for later, but it should be conducted early in the change management process because it provides an excellent benchmark that's needed to measure improvement. We recommend that all the employees and managers have the opportunity to take the survey and that it be repeated every eighteen to twenty-four months.

Typically the surveys are divided into sections that cover:

- Overall organization
- Job itself
- Management
- Performance appraisal
- Employee development
- Job demands
- Productivity
- Compensation and benefits
- Written comments

> **"Life is like an ever-shifting kaleidoscope—a slight change, and all patterns alter."**
> **—Sharon Salzberg**
> **Insight Meditation Society**

An opinion survey can consist of thirty to 120 questions. It should include about thirty core questions that all opinion surveys should use. These core questions are used to develop key indicators such as:

- Morale index
- Management index
- Trust index
- Satisfaction index
- Performance appraisal index

Typical core questions for the morale index for a hypothetical organization, named "ABC Inc.," would be:

- *ABC Inc. as an organization.* How would you rate ABC Inc. as an organization to work for, compared to other organizations you know about (reputation, salary, type of work, management, recognition, etc.)?
- *Overall satisfaction.* Considering everything, how would you rate your overall satisfaction with ABC Inc. (culture, job assignment, management, stress level, job demands, etc.)?
- *Job liking/kind of work.* How do you like your job—the kind of work you do?
- *Salary rating.* How would you rate your salary considering what you could get for the same kind of work in other organizations?
- *Job by immediate manager.* How good a job do you think your immediate manager and/or supervisor is doing?
- *Trust in management.* To what extent can you trust ABC Inc.'s management team?
- *Opportunity for a better job.* How would you rate your opportunity to move into a better position at ABC Inc.?
- *Productivity.* To what extent does unnecessary work interfere with your productivity?

To determine the morale index, you would add up the averages of all the individual questions (using a five-point scale) and divide the total score by the number of questions.

The opinion survey should be structured so that each natural work team of more than eight people gets feedback related to the input of its members. This allows the teams to prepare corrective action plans for their specific concerns and for questions that they answered statistically more negatively than the rest of the organization did. The executive team should develop action plans for all questions with responses that are average or below average. They should also develop plans that will lead to a minimum of 10 percent improvement by the next opinion survey.

ACTIVITY 1.2—DEVELOP KEY BUSINESS DRIVERS' VISION STATEMENTS

This set of vision statements is very different from the vision statement that we are used to seeing for the total organization. The total organization's vision statements include phrases such as, "We will be the biggest and most advanced organization in our field." They're usually very general and for most organizations they are unattainable, for only one organization can be the "biggest" or the "best." In contrast, the business drivers' vision statements are controllable by the organization's managers and employees. They're statements that should drive the strategic plan and the behaviors of the people who make up the organization. It's even acceptable to have a vision statement that says, "We're happy with the way things are for this business driver and will not be changing it for the next three years."

> **"Vision without action is a dream, action without vision just passes time, vision with action changes the world."**
> **—Joel Barker**
> **Author, *Future Edge***

To develop the key business drivers' statements, the executive team should hold a two-day meeting off-site in a sterile environment where no one will be interrupted by telephone calls. The time spent during the day discussing visions for the organization is important, but equally important are evening activities where members of the executive team can socialize and informally interact.

Preliminary Management Leadership and Support Vision

- Leaders inspire confidence through communicating a clear understanding of the company's goals and objectives and by empowering all employees to participate in accomplishing the desired results.
- Leaders encourage, coach, mentor, and provide the tools, training, and time to do the job right every time.

> **"The bottom line is that change is only climactic when you don't know where you're going."**
> **—Celestial Seasonings Inc.**

These preliminary vision statements reflect the way management interprets the data it has and the way it would like the organization's environment to evolve. But management makes up only a small part of the people who are affected by these vision statements. At least three other stakeholders need to influence these vision statements. They are:

- The customer
- The employee
- The supplier and alliance partner

> **"Companies confuse propaganda with communication. They think if they just talk at people enough, people will embrace the change. That's a big mistake, because you need two-way communication so people can find a way to get committed to the change."**
> **—Lance Dublin**
> **President and CEO, Lance Dublin Consulting**

So that the total organization is involved, each member of the executive team should pull together focus groups of his or her employees and present the preliminary vision statements to them, asking questions such as:

- Is this the type of environment you'd want to live in?
- Is this different from today's environment?
- Do you understand the vision statement and what each word means?
- How could it be improved?
- Do you think it's achievable?
- What would keep us from achieving it?

Procurement should ask major suppliers to attend a focus-group meeting where all of the vision statements are reviewed, but most of the supplier focus-group time would be directed at the supplier partnership vision statements. Sales and marketing should do the same thing for their customers, with particular emphasis on presenting the customer partnership vision statements. With both the suppliers and the customers, it is better to review the vision statements with too many, rather than with too few.

When the results of the focus-group meetings are available, the executive team holds a second meeting to develop the final vision statement. At this meeting the executives represent their functions, rather than themselves. Based upon my experience in this process, I can say that the result of the second meeting is a final set of vision statements that are significantly different from the preliminary vision statements. The following is the typical vision statement for leadership and support as it was modified after being reviewed by the employees:

Final Management Leadership and Support Vision

- Managers are leaders who inspire confidence through communication of a clear understanding of the company's goals and objectives and empower all employees to be leaders in accomplishing the desired results.
- Leaders lead by example. They encourage, motivate, coach, mentor, and provide the necessary tools.

This cycle really sets the stage for change. In most organizations, this is the first time that the employees have ever been asked to help define the environment that they'll be living in. This is the driving factor for the strategic plan. The fact that the final vision statement usually differs from the preliminary version shows the employees that management is listening to them and responding to their needs. It doesn't seem to make any difference if any one individual's suggestion gets into the final version or not. The fact that the employees' ideas were reflected in the final version helps to build trust in the management team. This cycle also sets very high expectations in the employees' minds and they will look forward to the change.

> **"If we did all the things we are capable of doing, we would literally astound ourselves."**
> **—Thomas Edison**

Typical Vision Statement for Leadership and Support

The following are typical final vision statements for leadership support, operating processes, and culture.

"Management fosters an environment of open communications where opinions and suggestions are encouraged and valued: Visions, plans, and priorities are shared throughout the organization.

"Management provides the necessary time, tools, and training for employees, which enables everyone to contribute his or her personal best toward the mission of the organization.

"Teamwork is emphasized. Decision-making is accomplished at the lowest appropriate level. Bidirectional feedback occurs on an ongoing basis."

Typical Vision Statement for Operating Process

"Major processes are documented, understood, followed, easy to use, prevent errors, and are designed to be adaptable to our stakeholders' changing needs. Employees will use these processes because they believe they're more effective and efficient than other options. Technology is effectively used to handle routine, repetitive, time-consuming activities, and reduce bureaucracy from the process."

Typical Vision Statement for Culture

"Our culture is built upon mutual trust and respect, integrity, professionalism, accountability, and commitment to shared vision, mission, values, and responsibilities that promotes receptiveness to new ideas, open and effective communication, healthy interpersonal relationships, and recognition of excellence."

> **"The 'hard' stuff is easy—it's the 'soft' stuff that's so hard to change."**
> **—Fred Smith**
> **Founder and CEO,**
> **Federal Express**

Note: If the present-state (as-is state) statement and the future-state vision statement are the same, you can skip phases 2 and 3 for that business driver because there's no perceived need for change.

ACTIVITY 1.3. DEVELOP PERFORMANCE IMPROVEMENT GOALS

The executive team should now define how it will measure success for the improvement change effort. Every executive has expectations of what should be accomplished in his or her function and in the organization as a whole. To guide the change planning cycle, the executive team needs to focus on setting goals for only a few critical organizational measurements. For example:

- Return on investment
- Customer satisfaction
- Response time
- Value added per employee
- Market share
- Error-free performance
- Dollars saved
- Morale index

You should always set SMART goals:

- **S**pecific
- **M**easurable
- **A**ccepted and agreed
- **R**eality-based
- **T**ime-phased

Figure 2.3 GROW Model

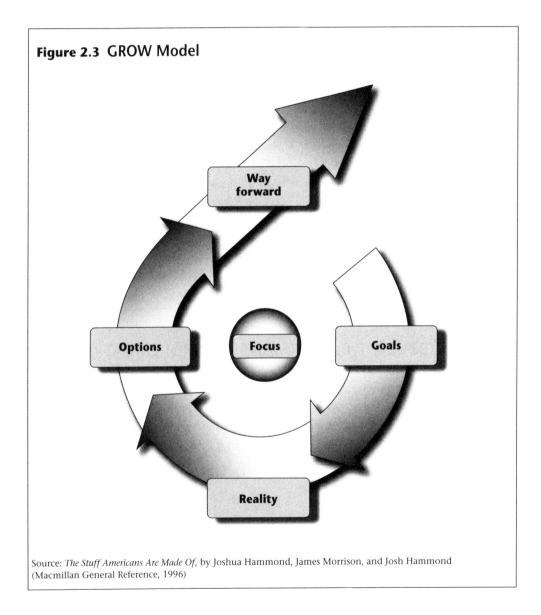

Source: *The Stuff Americans Are Made Of*, by Joshua Hammond, James Morrison, and Josh Hammond (Macmillan General Reference, 1996)

The goals should be challenging but not overwhelming. Think of goals as the start of the GROW Model:

Goals—Set goals that are meaningful and can be accomplished within the time allotted.

Reality—Understand the real world that you exist in. A clear view of the current reality can define new options.

Options—Look at all options before you set a course of action.

Way forward—Be very specific in defining your action plans. Be sure the new step is doable and the organization is in tune with the plan.

The executive team should select three to six organizationwide measurements and set yearly goals for them. The change process will be designed around these goals, and how aggressive these improvement performance goals are will have a great impact on the ultimate design of the change process. Figure 2.4 is a typical example of an organization's performance goals.

Figure 2.4 Performance Goals Example

Measurement	Year					
	0	1	2	3	4	5
1. Customer satisfaction	60%	65%	75%	80%	85%	95%
2. Return on investment from TIM		1:1	4:1	15:1	30:1	40:1
3. ROI from the change process		2:1		5:1		10:1
4. Defect rate improvement		2X		10X		100X
5. Value-added/employee in $1,000	45	50	65	70	75	80
6. New product cycle time in months	53	53		30		15

ACTIVITY 1.4. DEFINE DESIRED BEHAVIORS AND HABIT PATTERNS

The first step in changing the organization's personality is developing a set of vision statements. If they're worthwhile and are embraced by management and employees alike, the individual's feelings and thought patterns will begin to change. If the organization and the individuals involved are rewarded personally and socially as these new feelings are embraced, through time they'll transform into normal behavior and/or habit patterns. For example, if part of your management support vision statement was to "empower your employees at all levels," this part of the vision could first be reflected in your employees as they begin to believe that they don't have to get management approval to take action on unplanned events. They'd begin to gain confidence that they could make the right decisions in many cases without management's help. With time and continuing management support, they'll begin to feel confident that they'll not be hurt because they make a "bad" decision, and their behavior patterns will change. More and more, they'll take the needed action, often telling management after the fact about the problem and how it was handled. They will start to come to management, explaining how they're going to correct the problem instead of asking management how to solve it. Positively reinforced behavior and actions become habits. At this point, these special patterns become a natural pattern. "It's just the way we do things around here; it's nothing special."

For every vision statement, you should prepare a list of habits and behaviors that would exist in the organization if the vision were realized. To accomplish this, the executive team may decide to focus on key words or phrases in the vision statements, or on the vision statements as a whole. Typical key words or phrases that might be included in your vision statements are:

- Empowered employees
- Customer-driven
- Process focus
- Streamlined operations
- Quality first
- Technology-driven

Using "empowered employees" as a key phrase, the following is a list of some of the behaviors and patterns that would be observed in an empowered workforce:

- Self-managed work teams are used effectively.
- Wild ideas are encouraged and discussed.
- Unsolicited recommendations and suggestions are turned in often.
- Business information is readily available to all employees.
- Management defines results expected, not how to get them.
- Decisions are made quickly and at lower levels.
- Second-guessing decreases.
- People define their work process and time schedules.

Now the executive team needs to select key behavior and habit patterns and establish a way of measuring how they're changing within the organization. For example:

- You could measure self-managed work teams by the percentage of people who are part of these teams.
- You could measure the degree to which wild ideas are encouraged and discussed by reviewing the brainstorming lists to determine what percentage of the items stretch the imagination.

- You could measure how often unsolicited recommendations and suggestions are turned in by the number of performance improvement ideas and suggestions that are turned in per eligible employee.

Using this type of thought pattern generates a very extensive list of behavior and habit pattern measurements, many of which aren't being measured in most organizations. The executive team should include many of them when creating the change management behavioral measurement plan.

> "Change occurs when an individual or group learns and adopts new ways of behaving."
>
> —HJH

CHAPTER III

PHASE 2—DEFINING WHAT THE ORGANIZATION NEEDS TO DO TO CHANGE

"Whether you think you can, or think you can't, you're right."
—Anonymous

Phase 2 consists of three activities:

■ Activity 2.5. Develop the individual performance improvement management plans.
■ Activity 2.6. Combine the individual performance improvement management plans (total performance improvement management plan).
■ Activity 2.7. Develop a 90-day action plan.

ACTIVITY 2.5. DEVELOP THE INDIVIDUAL PERFORMANCE IMPROVEMENT MANAGEMENT PLANS

The organization has now defined the status of each of its key business drivers and developed a verbal "picture" of how it needs to change through the next three to five years. To define the action it must take to move from the present state to the desired future state, the organization needs to identify which present conditions have a negative impact (current problems) upon the key business drivers. Current problems must be solved before the key business drivers can start to change. Then the organization must define any additional roadblocks that will prevent the transformation from taking place. (See figure 3.1.) This list is prepared separately for each key business driver.

Definition: Transformation is the orderly progress from one state, condition, or action to another.

Organizations that want to eliminate the piecemeal, flavor-of-the-month approach to improvement are stepping back and looking at all their improvement options before committing to a course of action. It takes time up front, but it saves total cycle time, cost, and effort over a three-year period. It also produces much better results. Properly designed, it

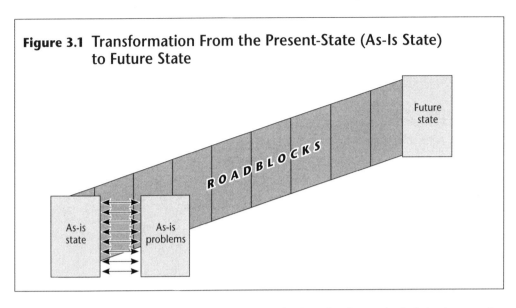

Figure 3.1 Transformation From the Present-State (As-Is State) to Future State

will create an organization that is creatively bringing out the best each employee has to offer. Work becomes a rewarding, enjoyable, exciting experience. The environment promotes a team spirit without taking away the individual's sense of accomplishment, achievement, and self-esteem. The excitement of belonging and achievement creates an electrifying air that snaps like lightning between management and employees alike, breathing new life into the entire organization.

Yes, a multi-year performance improvement management plan lies at the heart of every successful improvement activity, and not just for the large corporation. We reviewed Globe Metallurgical's "QEC Continuous Improvement Plan." Globe was the first small business to win the coveted Malcolm Baldrige National Quality Award. Globe's continuous improvement management plan contained ninety-six objectives, with multiple projects for most of the objectives and target completion dates distributed over a two-year period.

Factors Affecting the Performance Improvement Management Plan

An organization must consider many factors before finalizing the performance improvement management plan. These factors can be divided into two categories: impacting factors and influencing data. "Impacting factors" are things such as the organization's mission, values, performance goals, and business plans. "Influencing data" are things such as customer feedback, opinion surveys, poor-quality cost, competitive performance, etc.

Certainly the culture, environment, and current state of the organization have a major effect on the final performance improvement management plan. Some of the other things included in these considerations are: technologies, standards, desired pace of change, and competitive environment.

The proliferation of improvement tools has certainly increased the complexity of the change planning cycle. Philip Crosby's 14 steps, W. Edwards Deming's 14 points, Armand V. Feigenbaum's 10 benchmarks of quality success, information technology (IT) packages, Six Sigma, total improvement management, plus hundreds of others—many are similar in many ways, but they are all different in other ways. So what is the result? The organization now has more than 1,000 improvement tools to select from.

Difference Between Planning and Problem Solving

We find a lot of confusion between planning and problem solving. Americans are good problem solvers, but they hate to plan. Planning sessions constantly flow over into problem-solving sessions. It's important to separate planning from problem solving if the performance improvement management plan is to be completed quickly. Planning is upper management's responsibility. Problem solving is the responsibility of middle management, first-level management, and the employees. Tabe 3.1 shows the difference between the two.

Table 3.1 Planning and Problem Solving

Planning	Problem Solving
Define direction	Define solutions
Identify change areas	Implement changes
Assign resources	Use resources
Identify needed action	Take action
Highlight symptoms	Find root causes
Look at big picture	Focus on single issues
Short-term cycle	Long-term cycle

Individual Performance Improvement Management Plans

The executive team should look at each vision statement and develop a plan to transform the organization's key business drivers through the next three years in keeping with the vision statement. This performance improvement management plan must provide a logical transition from the present state (as-is state) to the desired future state.

Here are the results of one problem identification cycle for management leadership and support.

- Team members brainstormed to determine their major problems related to management leadership and support:
  - □ Confidence and trust in management

"Emerging technologies provide enormous opportunities to change business models—even entire industries."
—Joe W. Forehand
CEO, Accenture

- ☐ Communications—up and down
- ☐ Morale
- ☐ Fear of accountability
- ☐ Too much structure
- ☐ Too many policies and procedures
- ☐ Lack of individual goals and objectives
- ☐ Autocratic history
- ☐ Empowerment
- ☐ Tools, or lack of
- ☐ Pressure to produce for short-term results

■ Team members then brainstormed to determine the various roadblocks that would keep them from improving in the management leadership and support area:
- ☐ Wrong people in management positions
- ☐ Inconsistent communication
- ☐ Lack of understanding "role" in communications
- ☐ Need one MIS system
- ☐ Management philosophy
- ☐ Lack of established plan
- ☐ Lack of leadership training
- ☐ Lack of self-confidence
- ☐ No common leadership language
- ☐ No willingness to change
- ☐ Loss of identity "fear"
- ☐ Lack of commonality and community
- ☐ Selfish motives
- ☐ Identify autocratic views (inappropriate)

■ The team then combined the identified roadblocks to determine key issues that were causing problems and the areas that would inhibit the organization from correcting and/or improving them:
- ☐ Lack of detailed plan
- ☐ Strategy and financial plan
- ☐ "Scorekeepers"
- ☐ Time
- ☐ Loss of control
- ☐ Suspicion
- ☐ Inaccurate perceptions
- ☐ Unclear benchmarks

- ☐ Training
- ☐ Leadership skills
- ☐ Lack of efficacy
- ☐ Wrong managers/leaders/people
- ☐ No risk-takers
- ☐ No "buy-in"

■ They used the Delphi narrowing technique to identify the most important problems. The team worked on each major problem area; however, it wanted to identify the problems needing the most immediate attention and work on those issues first.

■ The problems and/or roadblocks are listed below in order of importance according to majority vote. The number to the immediate right of the statement (e.g. 8/4) is the weighted value given by the Delphi technique.
- ☐ Lack of a detailed strategic direction—8/4
- ☐ Lack of commonality—6/2
- ☐ Management philosophy buy-in—6/2
- ☐ Lack of "make it happen," results-oriented people—4/3
- ☐ Communication—4/3
- ☐ Lack of individual goals and objectives—4/2
- ☐ Lack of leadership training—3/1
- ☐ Lack of a common information system—1/1

■ Listed below are the major improvement opportunities they identified and for which they developed a detailed action plan.
- ☐ Lack of strategic direction in detail. "Road Map" to our company's goals and objectives.
- ☐ Lack of commonality "symptom not problem"
- ☐ Management philosophy buy-in
  - ● Make-it-happen people
  - ● Empowerment belief
  - ● Accountability
  - ● End-result–oriented

- ☐ Lack of leadership training
- ☐ Lack of individual objectives that support the organization's mission (bottom-up process)
- ☐ Lack of employee overall training

Now the challenge is to define which tools and/or methodologies will be used to negate these problems and/or roadblocks and take advantage of the opportunities for improvement. *Performance Improvement Methods,* a book authored by Kenneth C. Lomax and myself (McGraw-Hill, 1999), identified 1,119 performance improvement tools or methodologies. They vary from the very simple to the most complex, from brainstorming to supplier change management, from check sheets to Six Sigma, and from teams to total improvement management. If the current status is the same as the future-state vision statement, there's no need for any action plans and you can set aside a number of the improvement tools. (For example, if the present status of leadership and support is the same as the vision statement, you can eliminate more than 100 tools from your toolbox.)

These tools include teams, consensus making, self-managed work teams, and empowerment.

An effectively planned-for transition:

- Isn't abrupt
- Doesn't create morale problems
- Doesn't have schedule slippage
- Isn't uncontrolled
- Isn't unplanned for
- Doesn't create customer complaints
- Accomplishes desired results without rework

The executive team will then generate a list of today's problems related to the business driver under consideration and a list of roadblocks that will impede its change of state. When this is complete, the tools that affect the business driver under study will be reviewed. For example, in the management leadership and support category, 103 of the more than 1,000 improvement tools are directly applicable in bringing about this transformation.

The appropriate improvement tools and the list of problems and roadblocks are then analyzed to determine which tools will be used to correct which problems. In many cases, different tools are effective for the same problems. The executive team must study these interrelationships to determine which tool provides the best combined results in the particular environment.

Subsets of the 1,000-plus performance tools can be applied to each of the key business drivers. The team compares the situation that these tools are designed to improve to the list of problems and roadblocks that was generated earlier. Many of the different tools are designed to correct the same problem and most tools will correct more than one problem. The challenge is to select the smallest number of tools that will correct the largest number of problems. An effective way to accomplish this is to prepare a chart like the one in figure 3.2.

In this case the team elected to use methodology ten first because it was the only one that solved problem ten, and it also addressed four other problems (problems one, three,

Figure 3.2 Problem/Roadblock Relationship to Tools/Methodologies

Problems and roadblocks	Tools and methodologies										
	1	**2**	**3**	**4**	**5**	**6**	**7**	**8**	**9**	**10**	**Total**
1	X		X	X						X	4
2		X			X						2
3		X		X						X	3
4			X	X		X					3
5				X					X		2
6			X				X				2
7					X	X					2
8						X				X	2
9		X		X							2
10										X	1
11								X			1
12			X				X			X	3
Total	**1**	**3**	**4**	**5**	**2**	**3**	**2**	**1**	**1**	**5**	

eight, and twelve). They then selected tool four because it addressed problems four, five, and nine, which hadn't been addressed. Tool two was then selected to address problem two. Tool three was selected next, over tool seven, because it addressed problem six and three other problems. Tool six was selected to address problem seven. The last tool selected was tool eight to address problem eleven. The total tool set for this example is made up of tools and/or methodologies two, three, four, six, eight, and ten.

Once the tools are selected, a plan to roll out each of the tools is developed for each of the key business drivers. (See figure 3.3.)

Once the executive team has selected the appropriate tools, it will prepare a plan to implement each tool and assign an executive sponsor the responsibility for ensuring the plan is carried out. At this point, it doesn't assign priorities to individual tools unless they have some type of interdependence.

After the individual business drivers' performance improvement management plans are completed, the executive team should then review the performance improvement goals to identify which measurements the specific plan affects. The team should then evaluate how much improvement the specific plan will bring to the affected performance improvement goals. Although a number of performance improvement management plans can affect each measurement, the sum of the effects for each measurement should add up to at least the minimum goal for the measurement. If it doesn't, the individual business driver's plans

Figure 3.3 Individual Performance Improvement Management Plan

**Key business driver:
Management leadership and support**

Activity No.	Activity	Person responsible
1.0	**Teams**	
1.1	Establish task teams	EIT
1.2	Develop training plan and budget for EIT	Task team
1.3	Implement training plan	Division president
2.0	**Start departmental improvement teams**	Department manager
3.0	**Develop strategic direction**	
3.1	Communicate to management	Sam K.
3.2	Communicate to employees	
4.0	**Performance planning and appraisal**	
4.1	New appraisal process	Joe B.
4.2	Communicate plan to management	Joe B.
4.3	Communicate plan to employees	Division president
4.4	Implement plan	Management
5.0	**Measurement/feedback**	
5.1	MBWA	Division president
5.2	Employee opinion survey	H.I.
5.3	Feedback results	H.I.
5.4	Re-survey	H.I.
6.0	**Suggestion system**	
6.1	Establish task team	Sam K.

Time axis columns: Month (1–12) and Quarter (1, 2, 3, 4).

= Action   = Ongoing activity

need to be improved. And even this is usually not enough, because individual actions may often be designed to correct the same problem, so you get a double count. In addition, improvement estimates are often optimistic. You should have a 50 percent safety factor in your estimate. For example, if your goal were to get a 30 percent improvement in customer satisfaction, we'd like to see the estimated results of individual actions add up to 45 percent improvement.

The executive team should also evaluate each of the specific performance improvement management plans to ensure that they'll be conducive to the "desired behavior and habit patterns" previously developed. If the individual plans don't meet this test, they'll need to be modified.

ACTIVITY 2.6. COMBINE THE INDIVIDUAL PERFORMANCE IMPROVEMENT MANAGEMENT PLANS (TOTAL PERFORMANCE IMPROVEMENT MANAGEMENT PLAN)

When the team has finished developing the individual performance improvement management plans, it's time to combine the plans and set priorities for them over three years. This combined plan is called the "Total Performance Improvement Management Plan." The team should consider several things when combining the individual plans, especially the performance improvement goals that the organization has set. Some other issues it should consider in scheduling the activities in the combined plan are:

■ Availability of resources
■ Other activities within the affected areas
■ Holidays and vacation periods
■ Seasonal and/or new product workload fluctuations
■ Interdependencies
■ Organized labor interventions
■ Change management timing

Figure 3.4 is a total performance improvement management plan. You'll note that for each line item, a responsible person (executive sponsor) has been identified. In some cases, a group such as the EIT (executive improvement team) has been identified. It's always best to identify an individual rather than a group because there's more personal accountability when an individual has agreed to sponsor the assignment.

The single biggest mistake most organizations make is in trying to put a change process into place too fast. Great care should be taken to balance the improvement effort and the resources required by the other activities going on within the organization. Most organizations want to overcommit to the improvement effort at this point. In fact, it's much better

Figure 3.4 Total Performance Improvement Management Plan

Activity No.	Activity	2002									2003						2004				Responsible person
		A	M	J	J	A	S	O	N	D	J	F	M	2	3	4	1	2	3	4	
P	**3-year/90-day plan 4/19**																				H.I.–EIT
0.2	Develop plans for individual divisions																				EIT
BP	**Business process**																				
1.0	BPI									Cycle 1					Cycle 3						EIT/Bob C.
																					EIT/Tom A.
ML	**Management support/leadership**													Cycle 2					Cycle 4		
1.0	Team training																				EIT/Task team
2.0	DIT																				Dept. mgrs.
5.1	MBWA																				Division president
5.2	Employee opinion survey																				H.I.
3.0	Strategic direction																				Sam K.
4.0	Performance planning and appraisal																				Joe B.
6.0	Suggestion system																				Task team
SP	**Supplier partnerships**																				
1.0	Partnership																				H.I.–Dave F.
2.0	Supplier standards																				H.I.–Doug J.
3.0	Skill upgrade																				Bob S.
4.0	Cost vs. price																				Jack J.
6.0	Proprietary specifications																				Division president

☐ = Action   ▨ = Ongoing activity

to be conservative during the first year than too aggressive. Organizations already think their workloads are 110 percent of their work-force capabilities.

Another major mistake is putting the payback point too far out. The plan should break even within six months and show a good return on investment by the end of the first twelve months.

The total performance improvement management plan is the nucleus for a number of individual projects; a standard project manager approach should be used to manage these. At a very minimum, a project manager should be assigned to manage and control the change projects. The complexity of the total performance improvement management plan often makes it necessary to assign other project managers to manage specific parts. For example, individual project managers might be assigned to installation of a customer relations management system, including the required software, or a knowledge management system, both part of the total performance improvement management plan. Some of the tasks the project manager performs are:

- Define the project life cycle.
- Define the stage gates.
- Coordinate the budget and get it approved.
- Put together the project team.
- Develop a risk management plan.
- Develop a work breakdown structure.
- Define constraints and assumptions.
- Prepare the project scope statement.
- Track and report project status.
- Ensure that project objectives and schedules are met.
- Ensure that proper project change controls are in place and working.

To accomplish all this, the use of a project management software package is recommended. For simple change processes, Microsoft Project is recommended. For more complex projects within organizations that have a lot of projects under way, a more complete project management software package, such as Systemcorp's PMOffice, might be more suitable.

Change Management Plan

Now that you've pulled together the total performance improvement management plan, you've defined who will be affected, when they will be affected, and how they will be affected. It's now time to consider how the organization is going to prepare its employees to accept and even embrace the changes they'll be subjected to. This will require the development of a change management plan, which will be integrated into the total performance improvement management plan. This change management plan will be based upon the organizational change management (OCM) methodology discussed in chapter 4. At this point in the cycle, the change management plan will just be the skeleton of the plan. The real flesh will be added as the details of each activity and/or project are defined.

One of the best ways to start to develop an OCM plan is by holding a two-day, off-site change management workshop with the key targets (people affected by the change), sponsors, and organizational leaders. The following is a typical agenda for this type of meeting.

- Introduction/ground rules/expectations/objectives
- Why change?
- Cost of the status quo versus the cost of change
- Creating a shared vision
- Inputs and expansion
- Understanding the human response to change
- The change process
- Change management strategies
- Change management roles and responsibilities
- Synergistic teams
- Managing resistance
- Risk factors
- Conduct change readiness assessments
  - ☐ Role mapping
  - ☐ Sponsor commitment
  - ☐ Target resistance
  - ☐ Culture analysis
  - ☐ Change agents' assessment
  - ☐ Cost of the status quo analysis

- Transition management
- Transition strategy and plan
- Mitigation plan development

Applying OCM tools to software development

A typical software development progresses through four phases:

- Phase I—Design
- Phase II—Build
- Phase III—Test
- Phase IV—Deployment (implementation)

Figure 3.5 OCM Assessments, Planning Tools, and Training

	OCM Assessments, Planning Tools, and Training	Software Development			
		I	II	III	IV
1	Adaptation capacity audit	■		■	
2	Change agent evaluation	■			
3	Change agent selection form	■			
4	Change history survey	■		■	
5	Change knowledge assessment			■	■
6	Change project description form	■	■		
7	Change resistance scale		■		
8	Coaching styles inventory and guide		■		
9	Communicating change: announcement plan	■			
10	Communicating change: constituency analysis	■			
11	Communicating change: project analysis		■		
12	Communicating change: statement development		■		
13	Communicating style survey and guide		■		
14	Culture assessment	■			
15	Culture audit			■	
16	Expectations for a successful change project	■			
17	Focus groups tools*			■	■
18	Force-field analysis*			■	■
19	Implementation plan advocacy kit				■
20	Individual plan evaluation				■
21	Implementation problems assessment	■			
22	Individual error rate measurements*				■
23	Influence style survey and interpretation manual	■			
24	Landscape surveys	■			
25	OCM training for sponsors, agents, targets, and advocates	■			
26	Organization change implementation plan (OCIP)			■	
27	Overload index	■		■	
28	Pain management strategies: sponsor	■			
29	Pain management strategies: target			■	
30	Personal power survey		■		
31	Personal resilience questionnaire and profile				■
32	Postmortem*				■
33	Predicting the impact of change			■	
34	Preliminary implementation plan		■	■	
35	Process modeling*		■	■	
36	Process walk-through checklist*	■			
37	Rewards and recognition tools*	■		■	
38	Role map application tool	■			
39	Senior team value for discipline	■			
40	Simulation modeling*	■		■	■
41	Sponsor checklist	■			
42	Sponsor evaluation	■		■	
43	Synergy survey		■	■	
44	When to apply the OCM methodology	■			

*Use of this tool isn't limited to OCM methodology

Figure 3.5 shows how typical OCM assessments, planning tools, and training could be used during a software development and deployment (implementation) cycle.

ACTIVITY 2.7. DEVELOP THE 90-DAY ACTION PLAN

Now that the organization has agreed on a total performance improvement management plan, it's time to put theory into action. The rolling ninety-day action plan provides the organization an agreed-to, short-range schedule for putting the total performance improvement management plan into effect. This schedule will be divided into weekly segments, often with specific target dates. (Example: The project team will meet on the first and third Tuesday of every month from 9 a.m. to noon; or, the final report is due Frebruary 3.)

To accomplish this, you should develop a detailed, day-by-day implementation plan for any activity that starts during the first three months of the total performance improvement management plan. The individual assigned the responsibility for that activity should prepare this plan. These plans are then combined into a rolling ninety-day action plan. (See figure 3.6.)

At the end of each thirty-day period, the past thirty days will be dropped off the plan and thirty days will be added to the end. In this way, you'll always have a detailed view of what will happen in the next ninety days. After this, the ninety-day action plan becomes part of the work breakdown structure and is no longer a stand-alone document.

It's easy to see that the ninety-day action plan constitutes the activities that are included in the project management work breakdown structure.

"If you're afraid of change, consider the turtle—
it can't move if it doesn't stick out its neck."

—HJH

Figure 3.6 Typical 90-Day Action Plan

Legend: ▭ = Action   ▨ = Ongoing activity

Activity No.	Activity	4/5	4/12	4/19	4/26	5/3	5/10	5/17	5/24	5/31	6/7	6/14	6/21	6/28	Responsible person
							Week Ending Dates								
P	**Planning**														
1.0	**3-year/90-day plan**														
1.1	Transcribe EIT written plan														E&Y/KL
1.2	Draft 90-day plan														E&Y/KL
1.3	Mail draft to EIT and division czars														E&Y/KL
1.4	EIT modifies/approves plan														EIT/NCH
1.5	Return revised plan to E&Y														EIT/NCH
1.6	Revise plan as needed														E&Y/KL
1.7	Present final plan to EIT			X		A	I								E&Y/KL
2.0	**Develop individual 3-year plans**														E&Y/div. czar
ML	**Management support/leadership**														
1.0	**Teams**														
1.1	Establish task team														EIT/NCH
1.1.1	Identify needed training														Task team
1.1.2	Develop training plan					A									Task team
1.1.3	Establish training budget						R								Task team
1.1.4	Present budget and plan to EIT							A							Task team
1.3	Implement training plan								I						Div. pres.
3.0	**Strategic direction**														NCH
4.0	**Performance plan and appraisal**														
4.1	New appraisal process								R						RAH
6.0	**Suggestion system**														
6.1	Establish task team														EIT/NCH
6.2	Determine type of suggestion system														Task team

X = Review   F = Form   R = Report   I = Implement   P = Plan   T = Train   A = Approval   D = Done

CHAPTER IV

THE ORGANIZATION'S CHANGE MANAGEMENT METHODOLOGY

"You can manage change or it will manage you. The choice is yours."

—HJH

ORGANIZATIONAL CHANGE MANAGEMENT (OCM)

Before we can discuss phase 3—managing the organization's change process, we must discuss some of the change management tools and approaches that help ensure that the people who are affected by the change will positively accept the change project.

A methodology called organizational change management (OCM) is used to minimize the disruptive impact that change has on the organization.

Definition: Organizational change management is a comprehensive set of structured procedures for the decision-making, planning, execution, and evaluation phases of the change process.

"Managing change has an art and science all of its own."
—Ellen Florian
Author

OCM should be used whenever any one of these conditions exists:

- When the change can have a major impact on the organization's performance
- When there's a high cost if the change isn't carried out successfully
- When there is high risk that certain human factors could result in implementation failure
- When a project must be completed in much shorter time than usually is required

Change Is a Process

We can think of change as a real process, just like any of the processes that go on within the organization. It's the process of moving from a present state, or as-is state, through a transitional period that's extremely disruptive to the organization; to a future desired state that someone believes is better than the current state (present state). (See figure 4.1.)

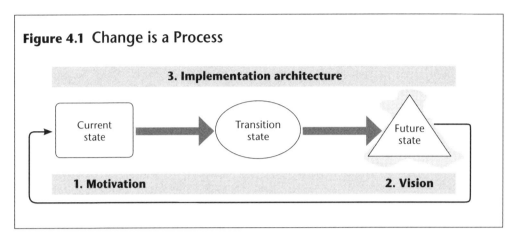

Figure 4.1 Change is a Process

Definition: Change is a condition that disrupts the current state. Change activities disrupt the current state.

Definition: Present state, current state, as-is state, and status quo are states in which individual expectations are being fulfilled. They're predictable states—the normal routine.

Definition: Transition state is the point in the change process at which people break away from the status quo. They no longer behave as they've done in the past, yet they still haven't thoroughly established the "new way" of operating. The transition state begins when the solutions disrupt individuals' expectations and they must start to change the way they work.

Definition: Future state is the point at which change initiatives are in place and integrated with the behavior patterns that are required by the change. The change goals and objectives have been achieved.

People are very control-oriented. They're the happiest and most comfortable when they know what's going to happen and their expectations are fulfilled. Keep this in mind.

For example, if I came home from a long trip at 11:30 p.m. and found all the doors unlocked and the lights on, but my wife wasn't home, that would be a change for me. It's customary for her to greet me at the door with a kiss. My expectations would've been disrupted. People resist change because they're dissatisfied about the disruption of the current state as much or more than they're afraid of the change itself. How would I react to this disruption in expectations? I'd call my son to find out if he knew where his mother was. I would wake up her friends to see if they knew anything about her whereabouts. I would call the local hospitals. I would be upset, worried, and unhappy. When change occurs and expectations aren't met, the 4Cs come into play:

- Competence
- Comfort
- Confidence
- Control

Change makes people feel that they're not competent enough to handle the unknown that comes with change. Change makes people feel uncomfortable because they're entering a world they haven't experienced before. Changes in a work environment cause people to lose their confidence. Before the change, they knew their jobs better than anyone else, but now they have to start learning all over again. Change causes people to feel that they have lost control over their lives and actions. From the individual's standpoint, the people who are making the change are controlling destiny. The person has lost control over his or her own life.

When the 4Cs are disrupted, emotions within the organization quickly head in a negative direction. Stress levels go up very quickly because people start to worry about what will happen to themselves and their friends. Productivity drops off as people make time to discuss what's going to happen and as they start to question whether they're doing the right thing. The organization becomes unstable as people start to react more slowly to the present process. People become afraid because they're uncertain about what's going to happen to them. This drives up the anxiety level of the total organization. Conflicts seem to break out everywhere. When people are worried and nervous, little things will send them over the edge. Little things that would've been ignored become the most important things in life. The slightest negative comment is blown way out of proportion.

Yes, change and the accompanying disruption of expectations cause the organization to tense up, to become high-strung and explosive. The child in all of us takes over and we become very emotional.

The focus of OCM implementation methods is on the transition from the present state to the future state. The journey of this transition can be long and perilous, and if not properly managed with appropriate strategies and tactics, disastrous. Each major improvement effort in the total performance improvement management plan will undertake this journey from present to future state. That's why OCM must be part of each of the total performance improvement management plans.

Determining When a Change Is Major

We can apply our first "best practice" to any improvement project by first identifying the pitfalls. Many organizations have a tendency to assume that every change or improvement project requires the same level of effort to put into place. In essence, they tend to repeat history: They budget the cost and time requirements for both the technical and human objectives as if all change projects were the same. The "best practice" you should apply here deals with accurately determining when an improvement project is going to be a major change for the people it affects within the organization. If it's a major change, then it's worth some special effort and special allocation of resources. Daryl R. Conner, president and CEO of ODR Inc., offers some guidelines to help determine if a major project needs special effort.

Factors to Consider

Essentially, there are three factors to consider:

■ Is the change a major change for the people in the organization (human impact)? A major change is any change that produces a significant disruption of an individual's normal patterns of expectation. To determine if a change initiative should be considered major, management should examine fourteen specific factors. The factors that disrupt expectation patterns are:

☐ Amount
☐ Scope
☐ Transferability
☐ Time
☐ Predictability
☐ Ability
☐ Willingness
☐ Values
☐ Emotions
☐ Knowledge
☐ Behaviors
☐ Logistics
☐ Economics
☐ Politics

One, or any combination of these factors, can cause the targets (people affected by the change) to see a change as major. Management must have a handle on the way employees perceive even what seems like the most insignificant change.

■ Is there a high cost of failure? What is the price associated with failing to carry out a specific improvement project (cost of failure)? It's imperative that management understands the consequences of failing to successfully carry out any change. Not only will resources be wasted on a problem that isn't solved or an opportunity that isn't exploited, but there may also be other implications, such as loss of morale, threats to job security, and loss of confidence in the leadership.

- What are the risks that certain human factors could cause implementation failure (resistance)? Questions that need to be answered include: Is senior management truly committed to this project, how resistant will the organization be, and does this change "fit" with the culture? Once again, ignoring any of these human factors can cause a project to fail. Later in this chapter I describe specific "best practices" that address a majority of these factors.

- Sometimes a project must be completed much faster than it is projected to be finished. Just adding resources and giving it priorities are often not enough. Even if the project is completed in a shorter period of time, it still needs to be accepted and implemented by the targets. This acceptance can take longer than the activities to design and implement the change. As a result, organizational change management approaches need to be used to minimize the acceptance cycle.

Senior management must be able to recognize these four business imperatives, which require a dedicated effort in managing the human and technical objectives if you're going to achieve success. Therefore, to leverage this "best practice," you should assess each improvement project that results from the adoption of a total improvement management (TIM) philosophy with regard to these three factors. That will allow you to accurately determine the level of disruption that the change will cause the organization, and how much time, effort, money, and resources will be required to ensure that it's successfully carried out.

When Should OCM Be Applied to a Project?

You can use the flowchart on the following page to define how or if OCM should be applied to a project.

> **"Change only occurs when individuals make a choice to change. We have to establish with people that there is less pain in moving forward."**
> **—William Bridges**
> **Author, *Managing Transitions***

PAIN MANAGEMENT

Next, we can discuss pitfalls. Best practice is to build the resolve and commitment necessary, not only to initiate an improvement project, but also to sustain that project all the way to completion. We've seen many organizations make the common mistake of strong, zealous initiation of improvement projects, only to have them flounder from lack of resolve to sustain the project to completion. Obviously, then, the best practice in this case is to build the necessary commitment to sustain the change with senior and middle management, thereby enabling the organization to manage the change process over time.

One of the main issues in any change project is achieving "informed commitment" at the beginning. You can apply a basic formula that addresses the perceived cost of change versus the perceived cost of maintaining the status quo. As long as people perceive the change as being more costly than maintaining the status quo, it's extremely unlikely that you've built the resolve to sustain the change process. The initiator of the change must move to increase people's perception of the high cost of maintaining the status quo and decrease their perception of the cost of the change, so that people recognize that even though the change may be expensive and frightening, maintaining the status quo is no longer viable and is, in fact, more costly. This process is called "pain management."

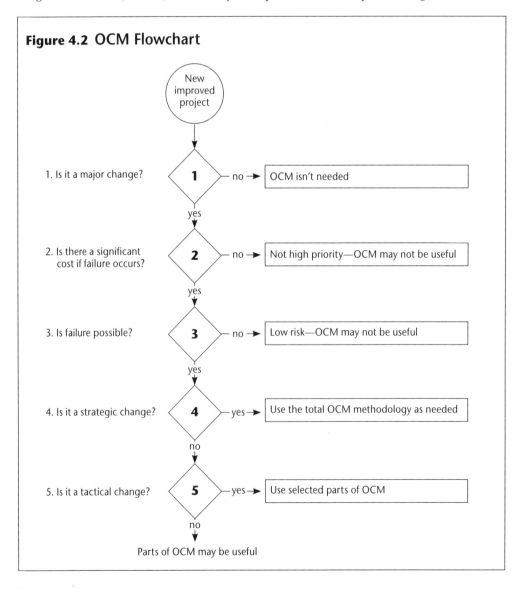

Figure 4.2 OCM Flowchart

Pain management is the process of consciously defining, orchestrating, and communicating certain information to generate the appropriate awareness of the pain associated with maintaining the status quo, compared to the pain that will result from making the change. The "pain" the initiator is dealing with isn't actual physical pain. Rather, change-related pain refers to the level of dissatisfaction a person experiences when his or her goals aren't being met or aren't expected to be met because of the status quo. This pain occurs when people are paying or will pay the price for an unresolved problem, or for missing a key opportunity. Change-related pain can fall into one of two categories: "present-state pain" (as-is pain) and "anticipated pain" (lost-opportunity pain).

"When one door closes, another opens; but we often look so long and so regretfully upon the closed door that we do not see the one which has opened for us."
—Alexander Graham Bell

"Present-state pain" (as-is pain) revolves around an organization's reaction to an immediate crisis or present opportunity, while "anticipated pain" (lost-opportunity pain), or, in other words, the pain if the change isn't made, takes a look into the future, predicting probable problems or lost opportunities. It's very crucial that management understand where its organization sits on this continuum of present-state pain (as-is pain) versus lost-opportunity pain (future-state pain). This understanding enables management to better time the "resolve to change." If you try to build resolve or commitment too early, it won't be sustained; if you try too late, it won't matter. Management has a wide variety of pain management techniques from which to choose. Some of the techniques being used by Fortune 500 companies include: cost-benefit analysis, industry benchmarking, industry trend analysis, and force-field analysis, among many others. When senior and middle management have accepted this process of timing the resolve to change, a critical mass of pain associated with the status quo has been established, and the resolve to sustain the change process has also been established. It's only then that management can begin to manage change as a process instead of as an event.

When it comes to the employees who are affected by a change, they usually have a good understanding of the present-state pain (as-is pain) in which they're involved. This may or may not be the true view of the present-state pain (as-is pain) of the total process. In fact, it usually isn't. But even if the employees have a true view of the present-state pain (as-is pain) of the process, they usually don't have any idea of its anticipated pain (lost-opportunity pain). For example, they may not realize that if they don't make a specific change, the organization will lose 50 percent of its customer base and the plant may be closed, so everyone will be out of work. That's why management must communicate to all the affected employees the present-state and the anticipated pain related to what's being changed. It's not enough to do it one time. It must be repeated over and over again, thereby reinforcing the need for the change.

Any project that results from the performance improvement philosophy will, by necessity, cause change in an organization. Applying this best practice is critical in beginning to mobilize support and understanding for the reasons for change, to help the employees let go of the status quo and move forward to a very difficult state, known as the "transition state." Managing people through the transition state to project completion requires resolve to not only initiate change but also to sustain it over time, with management continually communicating the necessity for change and supporting the actions required to bring it about.

It's important to remember that any type of disruption stimulates resistance. The individual's existing frame of reference (FOR) provides unconscious psychological security. You can break this strong commitment to the current state only when the individual's perceived pain in the current state is greater than his or her perceived pain (fear) of the transitional and future states. (See figure 4.3.)

Two factors determine the impact of the present-state pain. Each person has his or her existing frame of reference that defines his or her level of pain in the present state. In addition, each individual has a certain level of pain that he or she can stand before deciding to give up on the present state and embrace the change.

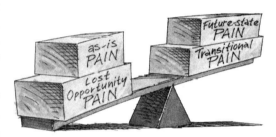

Figure 4.3 Pain Management

The first part of the equation is to generate enough information about the pain related to the present state (as-is state) that the individual becomes open to making a change. Next, you minimize the individual's perception of the turmoil that he or she will go through during the transition state. You can accomplish this by providing information about the implementation plan, involving the employee in the planning, and providing education and training for the affected people early in the cycle.

The last part of the equation is to provide a realistic vision of the anticipated state (future state). Too often we make changes without considering the fabric or organizational context of the action. Contextual leadership is a key part of OCM. It's the ability to provide a specific frame of reference about the change and its impact upon the affected individuals. This ability provides people a view of the change so that they understand what's going to happen to them and why. To provide this level of understanding, you must prepare four key documents related to the anticipated state (future state).

"The way I see it—if you want the rainbow, you gotta put up with the rain."
—Dolly Parton
Country music singer

- Vision statement
- Mission statement

- Operational plan
- Human attributes analysis

> "There's no such thing as the perfect solution.
> Every solution, no matter how good, creates new problems."
> —HJH

A vision statement should be broad enough to define the future state, yet specific enough to be personal to the affected individuals. It should be progressive enough to open everyone's eyes to what can be accomplished, but at the same time, it must be realistic. Unrealistic vision statements will get ignored, as will "ho-hum" ones. A good vision statement stretches people beyond their current capabilities without setting up false hopes and dreams that they can't obtain. The vision statement should be the stimulus that unites people and motivates them to embrace the change.

Additionally, a good vision statement will instill enthusiasm and capture not only the individual's attention, but also his or her personal desires, logic, and objectives. It's designed to bridge the gap between the individuals who are affected by the change and the organization's need for the change. The vision statement should address:

- Why the organization is making the change
- How the change will affect the processes
- What's in it for the affected people and the organization
- What behavioral patterns will be affected

> **"(In 2001) employees were ready to say, 'I am going to go where you lead me because I see we need to travel in a new direction.'"**
> **—Marie Eckstein**
> **Executive director,**
> **Dow Corning**

The vision statement should paint a picture of the future state to the degree that the individual can judge the amount of pain that he or she will encounter when the change is carried out. All employees realize that any change will cause future-state pain, no matter how good the intentions of the change team.

The mission statement also helps the individual to better understand the future-state environment and its pain. It provides an understanding of what must be accomplished if the future state is to be achieved. It will identify the human and technical objectives of the change.

The operating plan answers the question, "What's going to change?" It provides the work breakdown structure that defines how the change will be achieved.

The human attributes analysis completes the view of the future-state environment. It defines the personal attributes that will need to change for the change to be put into place. It will identify the need for changes in things such as:

- Values
- Beliefs

- Behaviors
- Attitudes
- Knowledge

With the completion and communication of these four key documents—vision statement, mission statement, operating plan, and the human attributes analysis—the individuals affected by the change will be able to evaluate the degree of pain they'll be subjected to when the changes are carried out. Now, based upon their own experiences and/or management-supplied information, the affected employees should have developed in their own minds an opinion about the pain they're being or will be subjected to in these four conditions:

- Present-state (as-is state) pain
- Lost-opportunity pain
- Transitional pain
- Future-state pain

> **"In the case of driving for excellence in these functional areas, you have to draw attention to the crisis to really make people take notice and say, 'Yes, we want to do it differently here.'"**
> **—Robert J. Herbold**
> **Former COO, Microsoft**

Based on their opinion about the pain they're experiencing and may be subjected to, they can decide to support the change, resist the change, or just wait to see how the change will affect them. If the combination of the present-state pain plus the lost-opportunity pain is greater than the combination of the transitional pain plus the future-state pain, they'll support the change. (See figure 4.2.) If not, they'll resist it and do whatever they can to make the change project fail.

Future-State Vision Statements

The other part of helping employees make the decision to jump is to paint a very clear picture of the future desired state. This vision has to address items such as: What would the business processes look like? What are the technology-, process-, and the people-enablers? People need to have answers to questions such as:

- Why is this change necessary?
- What's in it for me?
- Why is it important to my organization?
- What's the downside to the change?

Once we provide them a good understanding of the pain in the present state and a good understanding of the future state, the employees are in the position to weigh in their own minds the change's

Get a clear view of where you need to go

advantages and disadvantages to them. At that point they will decide to move forward or to resist your change initiative.

The Burning Platform

Daryl R. Conner originated the term "burning platform" to describe exposing the pain of the present state based upon a disastrous fire that occurred on an oil-drilling platform.

> **"They spent their time mostly looking forward to the past."**
> **—John Osborne**
> **Author, *Look Back in Anger***

"At nine-thirty on a July evening in 1988, a disastrous explosion and fire occurred on an oil-drilling platform in the North Sea off the coast of Scotland. One hundred and sixty-six crewmembers and two rescuers lost their lives in the worst catastrophe in the twenty-five-year history of exporting North Sea oil. One of the sixty-three crewmembers who survived was a superintendent, Andy Mochan. His interview helped me find a way to describe the resolve that change winners manifest.

"From the hospital bed, he told of being awakened by the explosion and alarms. He said that he ran from his quarters to the platform edge and jumped 15 stories from the platform to the water. Because of the water's temperature, he knew that he could live a maximum of only twenty minutes if he were not rescued. Also, oil had surfaced and ignited. Yet Andy jumped 150 feet in the middle of the night into an ocean of burning oil and debris.

"When asked why he took the potentially fatal leap, he did not hesitate. He said, 'It was either jump or fry.' He chose possible death over certain death.

"Andy Mochan jumped off the oil platform into the water not because it was a good thing to do, but because it was the best option he had. He jumped because the pain of staying on the platform (present-state pain) was much greater than the pain of falling fifteen stories into the water.

> **"Change isn't something you do by memos. You have got to involve people's bodies and souls if you want your change effort to work."**
> **—Lou Gerstner**
> **Former CEO, IBM**

"It's often very difficult to get people to move away from the present, familiar state and risk that the future state will be better for them and not just better for the organization. In this case, management must define and communicate that the change is not just a good idea, but that it is a business imperative. People will accept change if they perceive the future state will be better for them than today's conditions."

—Daryl R. Conner
Co-author, *Project Change Management* (McGraw-Hill, 2000)

As people face change, they react in different ways. Think of boiling water as the turmoil we face in this ever-changing world. If we have three pots of boiling water and put a carrot in one, an egg in the second, and coffee grounds in the third and let them all boil, the outcome will teach us something about how change affects different people. The car-

Motivation for change

rot went in hard but came out soft and weak. The egg went in fragile but came out hard. The coffee changed the water into something better. How does this apply to you? Will you give up, become something hard, or will you transform change into triumph? As the "chef" of your own life, what do you bring to the table? (Adapted from *www.accesschristian.com*.)

Change Prerequisites

"It is easy to come up with new ideas, but the really hard thing to do is to give up something that worked last year."

—HJH

Three prerequisites are required for change to occur and to be effective. They are:

- *Motivation.* The people who will have to change must be motivated to accept the changes in their work environment. We'll call the individuals who are the targets of the change process "change targets."
- *Commitment.* The change targets need to understand how the change is going to affect them. This requires that the change targets be provided a detailed understanding of how the change will affect them and their associates well before the change is carried out. This understanding of the future state is a key ingredient in creating desire to accept the change.
- *Implementation architecture.* The implementation architecture provides the bridge from the present to the future state.

"You have to make it clear that change is what the goal is, what your expectation is, and it is going to be meaningful in terms of its financial and organizational impact."

—Robert J. Herbold
Former COO, Microsoft

Change Management Communications

Communications to the affected managers and employees alike must start on day one of any project and continue well after the project is complete. You need to answer the following three questions for each person again and again.

The organizational change process must create strategic paths of communication to make a rational case for change and develop a sense of urgency related to the change. The more unpleasant the change, the more effort has to go into communicating it. If left on their own, people will blow both the bad and good news out of proportion. For example, if you're going to reengineer accounts payable with an objective of reducing cycle time, the rumor mill will soon have everyone believing that 90 percent of the staff will be laid off because someone heard that is what reengineering does. Change can lead very quickly to personnel problems if you don't keep the communication channels open and use them frequently. People always seem to discard good news when they hear bad news.

> **"Our criminal system knows you cannot force anyone to change. All you can do is present them with the options so that they can set their own course."**
> **—Daryl R. Conner**
> Co-author, *Project Change Management*

An ongoing flow of information about the change is critical to the success of the change. Keep reminding the employees of the logic behind the change and highlight its benefits. The project team members must be cheerleaders, focusing their discussions on how the change will benefit the organization and the staff. Management should schedule regular update meetings with all the affected staff to communicate the status of the change. Always tell the truth, even if it's unpleasant. Getting it out in the open is always better.

Bad communication builds high levels of resistance. Good communication breaks down resistance and builds resiliency. When things are changing, there are always more questions than answers.

The OCM methodology must address two different, but similar, situations.

- How change is affecting the total organization
- How an individual change will affect the people it has an impact on

Today's fast-moving, rapidly changing business scene puts stress on the total organization. It seems that even before a change is fully in place, another change is affecting the first change. Today, if we really feel comfortable with the processes that we're using, they're probably obsolete.

> **"If you can put in a culture that knows change is inevitable and an opportunity, not a threat, then I think you have the potential to have a company that can grow to a very large size."**
> **—Fred Smith**
> Founder and CEO, Federal Express

KEY CHANGE MANAGEMENT ROLES

In the organizational change management methodology, people are called upon to play five different roles. Often an individual will play different roles based upon the specific situation. For example, a manager may need to change before he or she can be a sustaining sponsor. Therefore, the manager becomes a change target before he or she becomes a sustaining sponsor. These are the definitions of the five change management roles.

Definition: Initiating sponsor is the individual or group with the power to initiate or legitimize the change for all the affected people in the organization.

Definition: Sustaining sponsor is the individual or group with the political, logistic, and economic proximity to the people who actually have to change. Often we talk about initiating sponsors as senior management, and sustaining sponsors as middle management, but that's not necessarily the case. Often sponsors can be someone in the organization who isn't in the direct management reporting line, but who has significant power of influence because of relationships with the people affected by the change, past successes, knowledge, or power.

Definition: Change agent is the individual or group with responsibility for putting the change in place. This person or group is given this responsibility by the sponsors. Agents don't have the power to legitimize change. They don't have the power to motivate the members of the organization to change, but they certainly have the responsibility for making it happen. They must depend on and leverage sponsorship when necessary.

Definition: Change target is the individual or group who must actually change. Many people don't like the word "target," but there's nothing degrading associated with the word. In fact, it's really more of an indication of where the resources, which are allocated to any specific project, must be focused to achieve successful change. If you really want to use a different name, "affected parties" also works.

Definition: Change advocate is an individual or group who wants to achieve change, but who lacks sponsorship. The change advocate's role is to advise, influence, and lobby support for change.

In most cases the project will define who will be the initiating sponsor, sustaining sponsors, and the change targets; however, you may have some choice about who will be the change agents and change advocates.

"A company needs a group of top executives to be champions for this approach. If they don't develop and nurture it, they will lose the ability to manage change at scale and speed made possible by advances in technology."
—Charles F. Kalmbach
President and CEO, DBM

Identifying the members of an organization who must fulfill these roles and then orchestrating them throughout the change process is a best practice, which organizations can use to greatly increase their likelihood of success with any specific improvement project. Once these roles are filled, management should maneuver these key roles to optimize each one throughout the change process to achieve successful implementation. To be effective in that task, management must understand the intricacies of each role, how they interact with each other, and how they work in an organization. The first thing that management must understand is that in all major change projects, key roles will overlap. When this occurs, the individual(s) should always be treated as a "target" first.

> **"Identify key people in the organization to spearhead the change. Choose them on their personal characteristics, not their place on the hierarchy. You want people who will be very strong supporters of the project and who have open minds."**
> **—Michael Tofolo**
> **Buena Vista Home Video**

Initiating Sponsor's Role

The initiating sponsors play the role of the organization's conscience. They ensure that the proposed project will have a positive impact on the organization and that it's a priority project within the organization. They serve a checks-and-balances function regarding the risks involved in the project and its chances of success. In addition, they review the project plan, approve the project budget, and are responsible for following the project and sitting in on phase reviews. Moreover, the initiating sponsors have the power to stop a project when they believe it's not going to meet its performance objectives.

The initiating and sustaining sponsors are responsible for establishing an environment that enables the changes a project requires to be made on time and within budget. The initiating sponsor may not be the person who originates the idea; that person is the initiating advocate. Initiating sponsors don't have to ask for permission to engage in change; instead, they keep the organization informed about what the change project is going to do, and they're held accountable for its success.

Sustaining Sponsor's Role

The sustaining sponsor is responsible for identifying targets within his or her assigned span of control, understanding the targets' roles in the change process, and working with the targets to break down any resistance that they may have to the change. The sustaining sponsor plays a major role in communicating the project's vision, mission, and objectives to the targets. He or she also helps develop an understanding of the present-state and anticipated future-state pain.

> **"Change management is a very difficult skill to master. It's easy to get up and give a speech or go to a seminar or put out a memo, but basically leading change is a day-to-day activity that takes a lot of work, a lot of energy."**
> **—Brian E. Becker, Mark A. Huselid, and David Ulrich**
> **Co-authors, *The HR Scorecard: Linking People, Strategy, and Performance* (Harvard Business School Press, 2001)**

Sustaining sponsors also provide a continuous flow of information about the project's status to the targets and feedback to the project team about potential problems that it may encounter in dealing with the targets. They often represent the targets' interests at project planning meetings.

One way to tell the difference between an initiating and sustaining sponsor is that the sustaining sponsor lives with the change after it's put in place.

Change Agent's Role

"Today, change agents must be facilitators of
the human aspects of change."

—HJH

Change agents are very special people. They must have excellent people skills and be able to understand and interpret others' behavioral patterns. These individuals weren't part of most project teams until recently. The project manager often played the role of the change agent without the required training. Basically, the change agent is responsible for making the change happen. The key attributes of an effective change agent include:

- Working within expectations set by the sponsor
- Applying in-depth understanding of how people and organizations react to the process of change
- Valuing the human as well as the technical aspects of change
- Identifying, relating to, and respecting the different viewpoints of sponsors, agents, and targets
- Collecting and appropriately using data regarding how and why people will resist change
- Helping build and maintain synergy among sponsors, agents, and targets
  - ☐ Communicating effectively with a broad range of people with different communication styles
  - ☐ Helping build and maintain appropriate levels of commitment to the change throughout the change process
  - ☐ Using his or her power and influence to achieve the goals of the change
  - ☐ Setting aside personal agendas, desires, and biases that might hinder the success of the project

In addition:
- Change agents shouldn't work harder than their sponsors.
- Change agents must be very effective and proficient at using all the change management tools.

It's very important to select excellent change agents, and they should be evaluated after each project based on the following:
- Is the person perceived as highly credible?
- Has the person earned the sponsor's trust and respect?

- Does the person demonstrate a high tolerance for ambiguity?
- Does the person thrive on challenge while avoiding stress levels associated with burnout?
- Is the person aware of the formal and informal power structure and know how to use it?
- Does the person have a good understanding of change management concepts and principles?
- Does the person have a high level of political support and credibility?
- Can the person effectively manage ambiguity and uncertainty?
- Can the person work within the sponsor's expectations?

Individuals who have the personal traits to be change agents should be trained in the change management methodology. If the individual doesn't have the necessary personal traits, select another. It takes a long time to develop the needed personal traits.

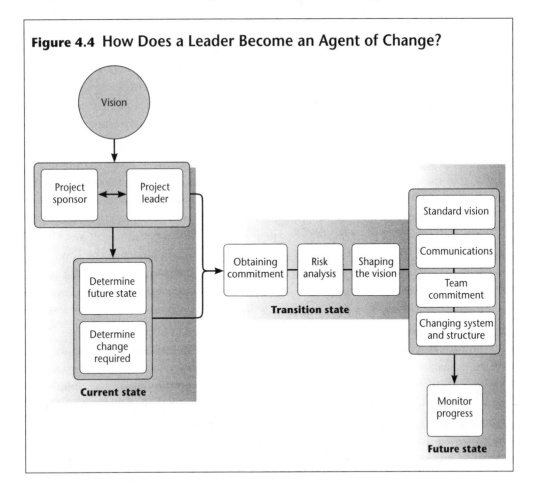

Figure 4.4 How Does a Leader Become an Agent of Change?

Preparing Change Agents in the Required Skills

We're living in a turbulent environment where change is accelerating dramatically in three ways: volume, speed, and complexity. This means that we can no longer manage as we have in the past. A possible pitfall in this area is that sponsors, often incorrectly, assume that those identified as change agents and advocates possess the skills necessary to successfully deal with human as well as technical implementation problems.

In today's unstable environment, it's necessary to have finely honed skills for managing and carrying out technical and human change. These skills are in very high demand, and special training is often necessary. The best practice for organizations is to build the capacity to manage change. To accomplish this objective, the change agents must come into the engagement with a different perspective. Part of the development of these skills is also a bit of a shift in mind-set.

When you look at agents historically, you'll note that they tended to have more of a technical-expertise mentality. Their primary focus and objective was to be sure that the change, whatever it might be, was technically sound; if people weren't able to use it, that wasn't the agents' fault. That mind-set must shift to a mind-set that sees the agent as a facilitator of change, that says change agents must be responsible for managing not only the technical aspects but also the human aspects of the change. This mind-set also dictates that the change agent should focus on the process as well as the content issues, with technology designed to accommodate human interests, needs, and values.

Truly effective change agents should be skilled in a complex combination of characteristics that can be brought to bear on a given change project. Successful change agents must have the ability to work within the parameters set by the sponsor and understand the psychological dynamics regarding how individual and organizations can modify their operations. Change agents must optimize their performance by placing emphasis on the technical aspects and especially the human aspects of the change. Change agents must be skilled in dealing with resistance. For them to understand that resistance, it's critical that change agents be able to identify, relate to, and respect the targets' and sponsors' diverse frames of reference. Change agents must also be the "cheerleaders." They must constantly strive to build commitment and synergy among targets and sponsors, at the same time being aware of and using power dynamics and influence techniques in a manner that reflects a capacity to achieve results in an ethical way. The bottom line is that a change agent must be professional, setting aside a personal agenda for the good of the change.

Success is ultimately judged by the achievement of both the human and the technical objectives. This change of perspective must occur if change agents are going to successfully manage the implementation of change projects. The change management skills within the organization are critical to the success of any change project. However, even the most skilled change agents in the world can't successfully carry out major change by themselves.

The other roles in the change process, specifically the advocates, must also have their skills finely honed and be prepared to use them.

The most important qualities in a change agent are that he or she be a visionary and a marketer—someone with good interpersonal and communication skills and someone who knows how to manage conflict. A change agent must have a spirit of inquiry. He or she needs to be able and willing to listen to people's true concerns.

Change Agent's Skills Evaluation

The change agent's skills can be evaluated using the change agent skill assessment instrument. This instrument is used to evaluate the behavior of the selected change agent. A typical evaluation leads to the following conclusions related to the project's change agents. The analysis defines the change agents as being barriers in the following areas:

"Only those who constantly retool themselves stand a chance of staying employed in the years ahead."
—Tom Peters
In Search of Excellence: Lessons from America's Best-Run Companies

- Their understanding of the human and psychological aspects of individuals, groups, and organizational change
- Ability to collect and use data to reduce resistance
- Ability to apply power and influence properly or correctly
- Ability to communicate effectively
- Understanding and respect for diverse sponsor and target perspectives
- Ability to synthesize different perspectives into mutually supportive action plans

This is a more typical result than usual. Most change agents aren't properly trained to do their assignment. The change agent's job isn't an easy one, but it's a very important one. It's often very difficult for a technical person to perform the change agent assignment along with his or her technical assignments.

Change Target's Role

Anyone affected by the change is a target. If the president of an organization is the initiating sponsor of a project to install a new labor-claiming system that will be used by all the research engineers, the vice president of resource and development is a target who must be convinced that the change is good for him or her.

The president has the responsibility for convincing the vice president of R&D that the change is good for the organization to the point that the vice president becomes a sustaining sponsor. However, just because the vice president becomes a sustaining sponsor doesn't mean that he or she is no longer a target. On the contrary, he or she will always remain a target; the president must keep dealing with the vice president to be sure that he or she doesn't have any doubts about the value of the projects the organization has undertaken.

Targets must be educated to understand that they're expected to accommodate change. They must be involved appropriately in the design and implementation process if they're going to embrace the change. Too many people think that targets are people who just sit there and have changes imposed upon them. They believe that they have no responsibility for ensuring that the change is successful. That may have been the case some time ago when a successful project, from the target's standpoint, was one about which they could say, "See. I told you it wouldn't work."

Today targets take on the key responsibility of providing input into the design that reflects the real operating environment. There's nothing like experience in doing the actual job to define flaws in a software or process design. The targets have the responsibility to maintain open minds, to give constructive suggestions, and to help with the implementation.

Good targets not only embrace change, they make it happen.

Advocate's Role

The job of the advocates is to persuade potential initiating and sustaining sponsors to support the project and to keep the sponsors' interest up to the level that's necessary to make the project successful. Too often a sponsor who is initially sold on a project loses interest or lacks the time to pursue it at the necessary level. When this occurs, he or she becomes dysfunctional as a sponsor. The advocate assigned to each sponsor is responsible for recognizing when this occurs and must take appropriate action to revitalize the sponsor.

Preparing Advocates in the Required Skills

To be a successful advocate, as with change agents, requires a special mind-set. Successful advocates must focus their attention on the sponsor(s) of the change and position the changes as being beneficial to the sponsor(s). Advocates must seek the approval of those in power and avoid at all costs wasting time or energy with people who don't have the power to say "yes." Effective advocates are results-oriented and are willing to accept nothing less than successful change. They're unwilling to simply adjust to the unacceptable status quo. Advocates must be confrontational and assertive and when faced with poor or declining sponsorship, they must be prepared to educate the sponsor, replace the sponsor, or ultimately to miss deadlines and projected budgets. ODR Inc. states that the advocate simply needs to follow five basic steps to be successful. These steps are:

1. Precisely define the change that needs to occur and how success would be measured.
2. Identify the key targets who must accommodate the change.
3. With each key target or target group identified, determine the initiating and sustaining sponsor(s) who must support the change.
4. Evaluate the current level of sponsor commitment.
5. Develop pain management strategies to increase and gain the appropriate sponsor commitment level.

When everyone in the change process knows his or her role(s) and has the skills necessary to fulfill those roles, successful implementation will be completed on time and within budget. Without the correct perspective and skill base, especially for change agents and advocates, the chance for successful implementation is nearly eliminated.

ROLE MAP DIAGRAMS

Change agent

Change ideas can die an early death if those who generate the ideas don't have the skills to gain support from those who can approve them.

Role assignments for change projects seldom follow a linear path through an organization. Working relationships can be highly complex and convoluted, with people often playing more than one role and frequently shifting roles once a change is under way.

At different times and in the face of different challenges, you may play the role of sponsor, agent, target, and/or advocate. Many change projects require you to wear more than one hat. It's not unusual for people to say, "I'm an agent for my boss, but the sponsor to my people." The issue isn't whether you're a sponsor or whether you're an agent, but in which type of situation you'll be a sponsor and under what circumstances you'll be an agent.

Definition: A role map diagram is the graphic representation of the key people, influential relationships, political realities, and organizational structures that are integral to the success of a specific component of a major change.

A role map diagram is used to provide a visual picture of the complex relationships that are required to successfully develop and carry out a change. It will help you to understand the flow of the change, and the related problems, issues, and opportunities. The purpose of the role map diagram is to:

- Identify the key people necessary to sponsor the change.
- Identify the primary targets of the change.
- Identify advocates who can influence the key sponsors.
- Identify the key constituencies affected by the change.
- Find the weak and/or strong sponsorships.
- Define the level of preparation among the advocates to influence their assigned sponsors.
- Build a common understanding of the issues, problems, and opportunities involved in carrying out the change.

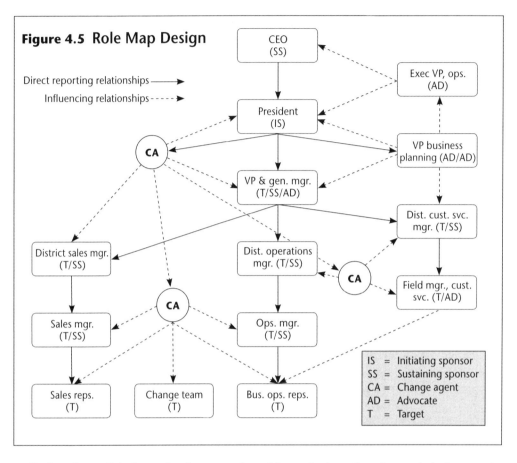

Figure 4.5 Role Map Design

Direct reporting relationships ⟶
Influencing relationships ┈┈⟶

CEO (SS)

Exec VP, ops. (AD)

President (IS)

VP business planning (AD/AD)

CA

VP & gen. mgr. (T/SS/AD)

Dist. cust. svc. mgr. (T/SS)

District sales mgr. (T/SS)

Dist. operations mgr. (T/SS)

CA

Field mgr., cust. svc. (T/AD)

CA

Sales mgr. (T/SS)

Ops. mgr. (T/SS)

Sales reps. (T)

Change team (T)

Bus. ops. reps. (T)

IS = Initiating sponsor
SS = Sustaining sponsor
CA = Change agent
AD = Advocate
T = Target

■ Define the political terrain that must be addressed when the change is being put in place.
■ Define the technical and human objectives of the change.
■ Understand the dynamics of influence that may affect the outcome of the change effort.

Figure 4.5 is a typical role map diagram.

The role map diagram for a change project should be developed early in the project cycle because it helps clarify the true nature and size of the effort as well as key constituencies.

When you're developing a role map diagram, always start at the bottom of the map by asking the following questions in this order:

■ "What people will ultimately be affected by the change?"
■ "To whom will these people look for legitimization of the change?"
■ "Who will be the sponsors of these individuals?"

(Be sure you look for informal leaders as well as formal leaders.)

Starting at the bottom and working your way up the role map diagram avoids the tendency to follow the formal organizational structure. Be careful not to confuse powerful advocates with the sponsors. People who are successful in achieving a change or convincing others that it's necessary are usually advocates and shouldn't be confused with people who have the power to legitimize the change.

CASCADING SPONSORSHIP

For each project, the change process starts when the initiating sponsor approves the project. Often the initiating sponsor doesn't fully understand the change he or she has approved, but the fact that it was approved legitimizes the start of the change activities. For all major changes, you must obtain the acceptance and support of the change from all the people in the organization who may not have direct contact with the initiating sponsor. To accomplish this, the initiating sponsor should enlist the help of the mid-level managers who have the power to legitimize the change with the first-level managers. Once the mid-level managers convince the first-level managers the change is good for their departments, the first-level managers will legitimize the change to their employees.

For example, if the president of the organization approves a labor-claiming system for R&D and product engineering, the president is the initiating sponsor. As the initiating sponsor, he has two targets (the vice president of R&D and the vice president of product engineering) to convince that the labor-claiming system would be good for them and their functions. Once the president has convinced them that it's the right thing to do, the two vice presidents become sustaining sponsors. As sustaining sponsors, the vice presidents must now convince the middle managers who report to them that the new system would be good for them and their departments. As the middle managers become convinced that the system is right for them and the departments that report to them, they become sustaining sponsors. The middle managers then have the responsibility to convince the first-line managers that the system would be good for them and their employees. When the first-line managers become convinced that the new system would be the right thing to do, they become sustaining sponsors as they have the authority to legitimize the system to their employees.

The process of transforming the levels of the management team from targets only to targets and sustaining sponsors is called "cascading sponsorship." (See figure 4.6.)

As you can see in figure 4.6, each level of management was first a target who had to be converted to a sustaining sponsor before he or she could start preparing his or her targets to accept the change.

Essentially, the way cascading sponsorship works is by starting with the initiating sponsor and working down through the different levels that will be affected by any improve-

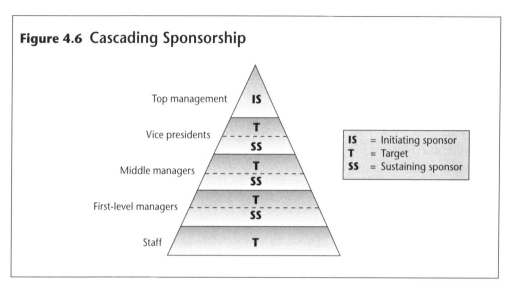

Figure 4.6 Cascading Sponsorship

ment project. Sponsors prepare the change agents to fulfill their roles, giving them the necessary skills to manage not only the technical aspects of the engagement, but also the human ones. The success of any improvement project starts at the top and ultimately rests on the shoulders of the sponsors. Sponsorship is the most critical risk factor in any change project. To have an effective network of sponsors, organizations undertaking major change need to adhere to five critical rules. Those rules are:

- Sponsorship is critical to successful change, so all sponsors must demonstrate unsurpassable commitment, both publicly and privately.
- Weak sponsors must be educated or replaced, or failure is inevitable.
- Sponsorship can't be delegated to change agents.
- Initiating and sustaining sponsors must never attempt to fulfill each other's functions. Initiating sponsors are the only ones who can start the change process, and sustaining sponsors are the only ones who can maintain it.
- Cascading sponsorship must be established and maintained.

Sponsors must also be sure not to just speak rhetoric about being committed to the change; they must openly demonstrate it. Sponsors need to develop a clear vision of the future state at the strategic and tactical levels and to pinpoint the appropriate amount of pain to move toward that vision. Sponsors must be educated to understand the effect the change will have on the organization and to empathize with what the targets are being asked to change about the way they operate. Sponsors not only need to be prepared to allocate necessary organizational resources (e.g., time, money, people, etc.) for successful implementation, but they must also be prepared to personally pay the price for success. Finally, sponsors needs to develop a reward structure that recognizes those who encourage the implementation process and discourages those who attempt to inhibit the acceptance of change.

It's very important to note that the transformation from targets to sustaining sponsors isn't always permanent. Managers who were convinced that the change was the right thing to do often change their minds or lose interest in the project. For this reason, the individuals who are targets for the initiating sponsor and sustaining sponsors remain their targets, and the sponsors must continuously reinforce the importance of the change with them even after the change is put into place.

Using a sponsor evaluation instrument, segregated by functional positions, will define the level of sponsor commitment to the project. Here's an example of an evaluation:

> "The sponsor's overall commitment was perceived to be insufficient to ensure successful implementation of the project. One of the managers sent out mixed signals related to his degree of sponsorship. He was viewed as believing that the change was needed and that he would track progress during the change process. On the other hand, he wasn't willing to champion the project and he was unwilling to reward the change advocates and to punish change resisters. In addition, he didn't understand the human impact and political or organizational cost of the change. He was viewed as being uncertain if he would be able to commit the necessary resources.

> "Another manager was viewed by all functions as being the most committed sponsor. He was rated as an enabling factor in all of the fifteen evaluation dimensions. It was unfortunate that he was situated in the organization in a position that had little impact on the total outcome of the project.

> "The third manager was perceived as an enabler by the IT function but was perceived as a negative factor by the other functions. She was perceived as not having a real understanding of the scope of the project or its impact on the other functions within the organization. In addition, she was perceived as being more concerned about the IT function than about the success of the project. She was also perceived as not having the required resources to implement the project on schedule.

> "The managers believed that they were more committed to the project than their subordinates would rate them as being.

> "The overall evaluation of the commitment of the sponsors was one of caution with more barriers than enablers. There was a strong need to develop effective change advocates to support the first and third managers."

Organizational "Black Holes"

Cascading sponsorship is an effective way to eliminate the organizational "black holes." These are the places in the organization where change decisions enter the process but are never heard from again. These black holes typically occur when there's a manager who doesn't sponsor the change, and, therefore, the targets beneath him or her don't adopt the change. There's little initiating sponsors can do to maintain the change at lower levels of the organization because they don't have the logistic, economic, or political proximity to the targets. The result is that change can't succeed if there isn't a network of sustaining sponsorship that maintains the integrity of the implementation as it moves down through all levels of the organization—hence, cascading sponsorship.

The term "black hole" is referred to by astrophysicists as a place in space where gravity is so strong that all surrounding matter and energy are drawn in, unable to escape. We all know people in our organizations who fit that definition. A black hole occurs whenever a sponsor stops supporting a change for any reason—be it logistic, economic, political, or for lack of resources, etc. It can be caused by:

- Bureaucratic layers
- Cultural differences
- Geographic distance
- Personal differences
- Budgeting issues
- Lack of time

A black hole exists because the cascading sponsor didn't build or sustain the needed commitment level from the target to achieve the change at his or her level. When faced with a black hole, the relevant sponsor can do three things:

- Replace the uncommitted manager.
- Prepare to fail.
- Educate the managers and put them on an improvement plan. Point out to them that such behavior isn't in the organization's or their best interest.

BUILDING SYNERGY

Definition: Synergy is the combined action of individuals or groups working together in a manner that produces a greater total effort than the sum of their individual efforts, generates more benefits to the organization than the resources consumed, promotes a higher future shock threshold, and requires less effort to change.

The next best practice to discuss deals with the idea of synergy—building synergistic work environments and synergistic work teams. Synergy is a very important concept when carrying out change projects. Synergy occurs when two or more people, working together, produce more than the sum of their individual efforts. Much has been said about empowerment, participative management, and cross-functional teams—all of which are very good ideas and necessary, but none are likely to be successful without a basic synergistic environment. A common pitfall is that management promotes the idea of synergistic output and synergistic teams, yet most fail to achieve them. The advised best practice is to enable sponsors, agents, and targets to work effectively as a synergistic team throughout the change process.

Integral to synergy is allowing people to work in a synergistic environment. Synergistic environments are open; there's no fear; there's five-way communication; and people in those environments really do think they can have some influence on the outcome of any specific project or business issue. To build this kind of environment and this kind of teamwork, you must first meet the two prerequisites of synergistic work teams:

- A very powerful common goal must be shared by these sponsors, agents, targets, and advocates for the change.
- Goal achievement requires recognition of interdependency: Sponsors, agents, targets, and advocates must recognize that the goal can't be achieved without working together.

Therefore, the best practice here is primarily to focus on making sure that those prerequisites exist. Once you confirm that they do, you can build a team and a process so that people can capture the potential synergy. With the prerequisites for synergy met, a group or organization can begin its journey through the four phases of the synergistic process and team development. It's important to note that all teams must go through this process—there are no short cuts. However, the length of time a team has already been together can affect how long it spends in each phase of the process.

These synergistic relationships are generated through a four-phase process. The four phases are:

- Interacting
- Appreciative understanding
- Integrating
- Implementing

Each phase is interdependent on the others, and individuals or groups on a team must demonstrate the ability and willingness to operate according to the characteristics associated with each phase.

Interacting

For people to work together effectively and synergistically, they first must interact with one another. If this interaction is going to be meaningful, people must communicate effectively.

At first, this task isn't easy and is one usually filled with conflict. This is what's called a group "storming." What happens is that the inevitable misunderstandings, which individuals are bound to have, go unresolved. This causes anger, frustration, blaming, suspicion, alienation, hostility, and possibly withdrawal. To stop this destructive cycle and avoid a total breakdown of the team development process, teams must move on to group "norming." Here the group decides on some basic ground rules as to how it's going to operate.

Appreciative Understanding

As important as effective communication is for successful change, something more must occur. Group members in a synergistic team effort must value and use the diversity that exists among them. This is a continuation of the "norming" process that occurs in team development. Valuing a different point of view can be difficult for some people because of the emphasis our culture places on rational, linear, left-hemispheric thinking processes that encourage critical analyses. This thought process can produce an "I'm right, you're wrong" attitude, whereas synergy dictates that people should support each other and look for the merit in another's viewpoint.

Integrating

Even though a team has passed through the first two phases of the synergistic process, it isn't yet sufficient to produce synergistic outcomes. Synergy is the result of communicating, valuing, and merging separate, diverse viewpoints. Once again, accomplishing this integration is extremely difficult because our culture doesn't teach and reward the skills needed. For team members to work through the "norming" process of team development and move on to "performing" the final phase, they need to develop the skills necessary to make integration possible. Specifically, team members need to:

- Tolerate ambiguity and be persistent in the struggle for new possibilities.
- Modify individual views, beliefs, and behavior to support the team.
- Generate creative ways of merging diverse perspectives into new, mutually supported alternatives.
- Identify issues, concepts, etc., that can't or shouldn't be integrated.

Implementing

Even the best plans and solutions are useless unless they're fully carried out. The bottom line for synergy must be the accomplishment of change initiatives. Synergistic events should culminate in well-thought-out, change-oriented action plans. The final phase in the synergy process is designed to build on all the momentum that the previous phases have generated and to direct that energy into completing the task at hand. This is the point in the team development process that teams actually begin to "perform." The key to success in this phase is basic management skills. As the capacity of individuals to grow beyond themselves (synergy) increases, it must be managed as any other valuable resource would.

Most implementation problems are the result of non-synergistic behavior. This behavior can be attributed to human nature and bad habits. Fortunately, if a team follows the guidelines developed to create synergy and effective team development, successful implementation will be the result.

RESISTANCE TO CHANGE

> **"The tough part is that many times you've got to change before the real requirement to change is necessarily seen."**
> **—Art Collins**
> **Chairman and CEO, Medtronic Inc.**

Resistance to change is normal and you should expect it. Your "gut" tells you something different is happening. In reality, it means you're on the edge of new growth. The desire for stability is part of our biological drive toward survival, and, in fact, if there isn't some resistance to change, you should be concerned. Think of how antibodies attack an organism that enters the body. Resistance is the natural order of things. If you don't encounter resistance, then you aren't changing enough or your people don't care. Intelligent people will always ask, "Why are we doing this?" You don't want people who follow blindly like a flock of sheep. People's resistance to change is usually rooted in real and understandable concerns. Based on their experiences, people believe that organizational change creates winners and losers. Some people take advantage of the change process and move ahead, while others lose power, status, and even their jobs. Psychological barriers to change are subtle. They tend to be variations of fear—fear of losing their familiar ways of doing things, fear of the unknown, and fear of losing status.

The biggest reason for a high level of resistance to change in an organization is the organization's culture, which can be described as "an invisible, impenetrable shield holding on the old behavior patterns." Organizations that are tradition-bound and committed to following procedures have a hard time changing as fast as they need to. Standards such as ISO 9001:2000 just add to this problem.

You can define resistance to change as "any thought or action directed against a change." You should expect some level of resistance in any major change.

> **"The real cause of reengineering failures is not the resistance itself, but management's failure to deal with it."**
> **—Michael Hammer**
> **Author, *The Reengineering Revolution***

Because resistance to change is inevitable, it's important that we understand why it occurs and how to minimize its impact on the change process. Too many organizations don't consider how significant the impact of resistance to change is on the organization. Too often we believe that, if it's good for the organization, the employees will have to go along with it. The truth is that workers would accept change without question back in the early part of the 20th century when we tied people to their machines and paid them only for their physical effort. But today we have, and need, people who bring more than just their physical beings to work. Today's knowledge worker must understand why change is necessary and, once convinced that it's needed, want to actively support the change initiatives.

It's best to regard resistance as a normal, necessary first step in the change process. Because resistance is inevitable, accept it, deal with it up front, and get over this hurdle as soon as possible. This is best accomplished when a sensitive, mature, and sympathetic manager addresses the situation, taking the time to make each individual feel safe and eliciting his or her true feelings and concerns. People who need to change must feel secure. Resistance to change will crumble only if we have a high degree of trust in our management team. By involving employees in developing the individual change design and implementation plans, we can often transform a person from a resister into an advocate. The difference between resistance and support is very evident. The attitude of resistant employees is, "Let me tell you why it won't work." Supportive employees ask, "How can I help you make it work?"

Twenty percent of the people will be against anything.
—Robert F. Kennedy
Former U.S. Senator

The question is, what level of resistance is normal? Based on our experience, the following applies:

- 30 percent of the people will support change.
- 50 percent of the people are undecided or neutral.
- 20 percent of the people will resist change and often will do everything they can to make the change fail.

It comes down to this: People have to change or be changed. Gary Loveman, CEO of Harrah's Entertainment of Las Vegas, was once discussing a change that ended the marketing fiefdoms in the organization's different properties. He stated, "In the corporate marketing department I don't recall that there were more than one or two survivors." In other words, don't bother fighting change. You either fit in or get thrown out.

You can use the change resistance assessment instrument to measure:

- The individual's perception of himself or herself as a change target
- Management's perception of their subordinates' resistance to the project
- Employees' perspective of themselves as targets

Here's an example of a change resistance assessment that was conducted on one project:

- The overall results showed that managers perceived substantial resistance to the change project and that it was higher than the sponsor commitment level. This means there's a high probability that the project won't achieve its objectives on time and within budget because the targets' resistance is higher than the sponsor's commitment to the project.

■ People believed that the targets had too little involvement in planning the change and that there were inadequate rewards for accomplishing the change. There was a perception that the change was more costly than if the current state were maintained. The participants believed there were more change resistance barriers than enablers. People thought that the change was contrary to their personal interests.

■ There was a common understanding of why the change was important and necessary. There was a general trust in and respect of the sponsors and agents.

■ At the functional level there were very different reasons for resisting the change.

■ In one function where the assessment found the biggest differences between the sponsors and the targets, no enablers were noted. The main barriers were:
   ☐ Degree of input the targets had in planning the change
   ☐ Adequacy of reward for accomplishing the change
   ☐ The degree to which their current work patterns were considered in planning the change
   ☐ Their needs for security

■ In another function that was most positive about the change:
   The main barriers were:
   ☐ Level of involvement in planning the change
   ☐ Adequacy of rewards

   "The conventional army loses if it does not win. The guerrilla wins if he does not lose."
   —Henry Kissinger
   Former U.S. Secretary of State

   The enablers were:
   ☐ Compatibility with their own goals
   ☐ Belief that their jobs will be positively affected
   ☐ The provision of adequate resources to support the change
   ☐ The level of respect and trust for the sponsors

It's easy to understand how having this type of information can help the project team design the project in a way that greatly improves its chances of success.

In most cases management spends far too much time reacting to the resisters because they're the squeaky wheels. They're hard to ignore. As a result, management gives them lots of attention, most of which is wasted effort. We liken the situation to that of a small group of people protesting something outside the U.S. embassy. Coverage on the evening news convinces them even more that their cause is just.

Management and change agents should spend their time and effort with the 50 percent of the people who are undecided. It's much easier to move them over to support the change than it is to move the resisters. Resisters use a strategy of delay. Move fast with your

"You must be willing to let squeaky wheels squeak. Save your grease for the quieter wheels that actually are carrying the load."
—**Price Pritchett**
Author and chairman,
Pritchett LLC

changes. Resisters hate to see things move fast. You'll pass by their roadblocks before they have time to set them up.

Definition: Future shock is the point at which no more change can be accommodated without the display of dysfunctional behaviors. (A more thorough discussion will follow later in this chapter.)

The Organization's Personality and Cultural Impact on Resistance to Change

The current organization's personality and culture are huge issues that you must address to accomplish change projects. Because organizational personality and culture are difficult to understand and hard to measure and manage, they're relatively easy to ignore. Commonly, organizations ignore them or don't treat them as key variables when carrying out a major change initiative. Obviously the best practice is just the opposite. Senior management must realize how strategically important the overall organizational personality and culture are to the change initiative and work hard to understand and manage the impact they have on the achievement of improvement projects.

Corporate culture is the basic pattern of shared beliefs, behaviors, norms, values, and expectations acquired over a long time by members of an organization. Organizational personalities reflect the way the present management team operates. If an improvement project or a change initiative is consistent with that set of beliefs, behaviors, norms, values, and expectations, then the organization's personality and culture are actually enablers of that change. On the other hand, a change project may run fundamentally counter to the organization's personality and culture, making acceptance of the change much more difficult.

We're very clear about one thing: Whenever there's a discrepancy between change in culture and existing culture, existing culture wins. So, to apply this best practice to any change initiative, we need to understand whether organizational personality and culture are enablers or barriers to the change. If they are barriers, we must identify what the existing barriers are, why they're barriers, and proactively modify the change or modify the organization's personality, or some combination of both, to successfully meet change objectives. Only three options are available:

- Modify the change to be more consistent with the organization's personality and culture.
- Modify or change the organization's personality to be more consistent with the achievement of the change objectives.
- Ignore options one and two and plan for the change initiative to take significantly longer and cost significantly more than what you may have originally budgeted (this isn't really an option).

You must consider eleven items in performing a culture assessment:

- Leadership
- Teamwork
- Business
- Structure
- Communications
- Knowledge flow
- Management processes
- Motivation
- Decision making
- Performance appraisal
- Change implementation

Here are the results of a typical culture consistency analysis:

- The participants classified eight of the eleven items as barriers or near barriers to carrying out the change. The most significant barriers were current structure and the incompatibility of the current status incentives and performance expectations (i.e., the organizational structure and the rewards system). Only one enabler was identified: It was teamwork.
- Functions showed great variation. One function viewed all cultural items as barriers except teamwork, which it rated at the caution level. Another function rated decision-making processes, current management process, communication, current structure, and current methods for conveying change implementations.

The Importance of Frames of Reference

Definition: Frame of reference (FOR) describes a compatible set of ideas, theories, beliefs, feelings, values, and assumptions that allow meaning to be applied to a person's experience. It's an unconscious model for comprehending reality.

Facts and figures aren't important to the individual faced with change or being part of the change process. Management can say it's good for him or her and it can paint a rosy picture of the future state, but that doesn't amount to a hill of beans. The only thing that counts is the individual's perception of the change and how it will affect him or her. That's why change management methodology and the change management plan must consider the individual's FOR. The individual's FOR drives his or her perception of the change and how he or she will be affected by it. It's impossible to understand why people react as they do without understanding the FOR.

An individual's expectations drive his or her FOR. It's very important that the project team and management know and react to the FOR of the targets because it determines how they'll perceive and interpret the projects. People can reduce their feelings of uncertainty and gain a sense of control by correctly predicting their futures. The ability to develop reasonable expectations is a basic requirement for reducing fear and uncertainty.

ASSIMILATION OF STRESS

Change brings on stress in each person it touches. Every person can assimilate a certain amount of stress before breaking and becoming dysfunctional. The breaking point is called future shock. Each change triggers an immediate spike in the individual's stress level that's sustained for a time and then starts to decay as the individual becomes familiar with the change. (See figure 4.7.)

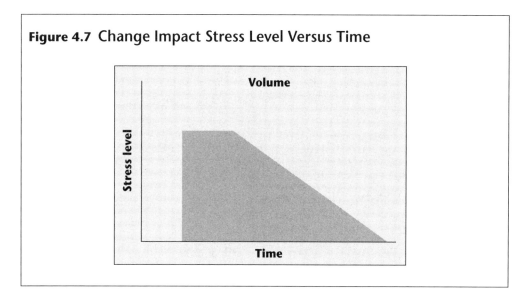

Figure 4.7 Change Impact Stress Level Versus Time

The height of the spike reflects the magnitude of the stress. This magnitude will vary based upon how the change affects the individual. (See figure 4.8.) The things that affect the individual personally—themselves, their immediate families, close friends, or relatives—have the biggest impact. They're called "me-type" changes or "micro-type" changes. Some good examples of me-type changes are death in the family, a divorce, or assignment to a new job. The things that affect only the individual, the group that he or she works with, and other institutions with influence (e.g., workplace, church, schools, or associations) have a moderate level of associated stress. They're called "us-type" changes or "organizational-type" changes. For example, a new manager is appointed to the department or the department is moving to a different place.

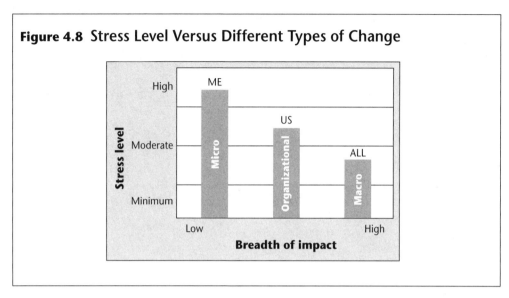

Figure 4.8 Stress Level Versus Different Types of Change

Changes that affect a large constituency or all of humanity have the lowest level of associated stress. They're called "everyone-type" changes or "macro-type" changes. For instance, when a new president is assigned to the company, a new product is rolled out, or a new appraisal system is put in place. (See figure 4.9.)

Micro change is when "I" must change. Organizational change is when "we" must change. Macro change is when "everyone" must change.

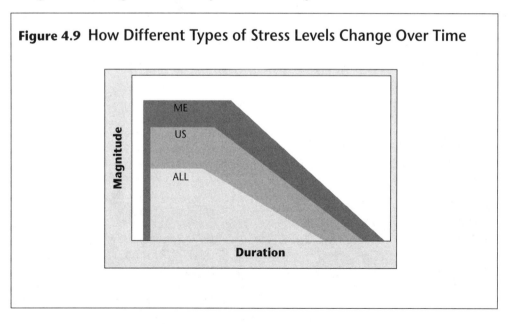

Figure 4.9 How Different Types of Stress Levels Change Over Time

Assimilating change involves not only the effort necessary to deal with what's causing the change (new technologies, reorganization, new processes) but also the short-term and long-term implications of change (shifting power bases, need to learn new skills, formation of new relationships, establishment of new expectations).

Assimilating change is costly to any organization. Assimilation involves:

- Intellectual energy
- Psychological energy
- Physical energy
- Personal risk
- Relationship risk
- Professional risk
- Economic risk

Future Shock

Definition: Future shock is the point at which people can no longer assimilate change without displaying dysfunctional behaviors.

When future shock occurs, it paralyzes the organization. Think of a deer that stops in its tracks when a headlight shines on it. Each individual has a unique capability for withstanding the stress related to change. This capability is measured in the number of assimilation points required to adjust to the change. The dysfunctional performance of future shock occurs when the total assimilation (stress demands) exceeds the individual's assimilation

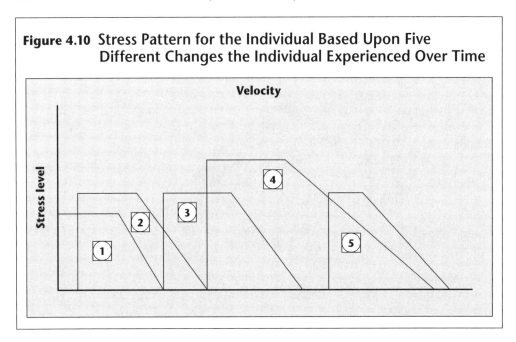

Figure 4.10 Stress Pattern for the Individual Based Upon Five Different Changes the Individual Experienced Over Time

capabilities. We liken it to an employee carrying a two-gallon container from one point to another. You pour "one gallon of stress" into the container and it gets heavier, but the employee is still able to carry it. Add another three-quarters of a gallon and the employee is still able to perform the task. But if you add another half gallon the container overflows, getting the employee wet, so that he or she drops the container, adding to the mess and stopping all progress.

That's exactly what happens to people and their reaction to change. Once they get near the future-shock point, even the smallest change can make them dysfunctional. We must remember that future shock occurs based not on a single change but upon the accumulated stresses that occur from all the changes that affect the individual at work and outside of work. This doesn't mean that a single change can't drive an individual into future shock. Some of the me-type changes are three-gallon changes—for example, a death in the family, a divorce, or being reassigned to a lesser job against one's will.

Figure 4.10 shows a stress pattern for an individual based upon five different changes that the individual experiences over time.

None of these changes is big enough to drive the individual into future shock by itself, but the individual can't treat them as disjointed incidences, as he or she is affected by the combined stress of all five changes.

Figure 4.11 indicates the combined stress pattern for the five changes. You'll note that change number four drives the individual into future shock and he or she remains there for a long time.

Let's assume that future shock occurs whenever an individual accumulates a total of 1,000 or more assimilation points at one time. The following would be typical assimilation points for different types of changes:

- Worldwide nuclear waste problem—macro-level change—for a peak of 100 points
- Environmental pollution—macro-level change—for a peak of 125 points
- New product release—organizational-level change—for a peak of 400 points
- New department manager—organizational-level change—for a peak of 600 points
- New technology—organizational-level change—for a peak of 400 points
- Major acquisition—organizational-level change—for a peak of 600 points
- Building a new culture—organizational-level change—for a peak of 900 points
- Major medical problem—micro-level change—for a peak of 1,200 points
- Divorce—micro-level change—for a peak of 1,500 points

You'll note that each micro-level change drives the individual into future shock by itself. Combining the normal macro-level changes of concern over the environmental pollution production project (125 points) with the organizational-level changes of building a new culture (900 points) could drive an organization into future shock.

Figure 4.11 Combined Stress Pattern for Five Changes' Combined Stress Levels

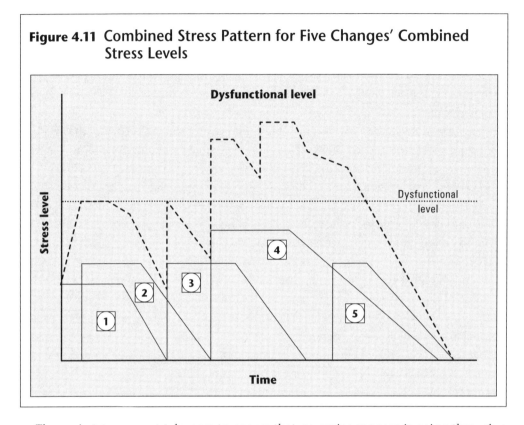

The project team must take care to ensure that no major sponsor is going through a severe personal problem at the time he or she needs to support the project.

The question is: "How do you keep the organization or the individual employee from going into future shock?" You have only six alternatives, all of which may be used simultaneously. They are:

- *Make fewer changes.* This is often difficult, and in the future we'll be called upon to make more and more rapid changes to keep pace with changing customer requirements.

- *Minimize the number of me-type changes.* The me-type changes have the biggest impact on the individual employee. Don't shuffle managers or departments around unless there's a good cost justification.

- *Reduce the duration of stress.* You can reduce the time it takes the individual from first hearing about the change to accepting the change by communicating the change to the employee based upon the employee's viewpoints and concerns.

- *Stay in tune with personal-change stresses that key people go through inside and outside the organization.* If a key individual within a change project is going through severe emotional stress outside of the organization, it's usually best to reschedule the change activity to a time when he or she has absorbed the outside stress factors.

■ *Decrease the degree of stress related to each change.* This is a magnitude issue. You can often lower the magnitude of stress by involving individuals in the design stage of a change project. When the employee has input of ideas and can affect the final design of the project, you can greatly reduce the emotional fear and stress related to the project.

■ *Increase the amount of stress related to the change that an individual or organization can endure before it goes into future shock and becomes dysfunctional.* You can accomplish this by building the resiliency within the organization.

EMOTIONAL RESPONSE CYCLES

Another very important tool in our arsenal of change management tools is emotional response cycles. Basically, every employee goes through two response cycles as a result of change. They are:

■ Positive response cycle
■ Negative response cycle

The positive response cycle is the cycle that individuals go through when they view a change as being positive for themselves and the organization. It's made up of five states. (See figure 4.12.)

1. Uninformed optimistic state (certain)
2. Uninformed pessimistic state (doubtful)
3. Hopeful realistic state (hopeful)

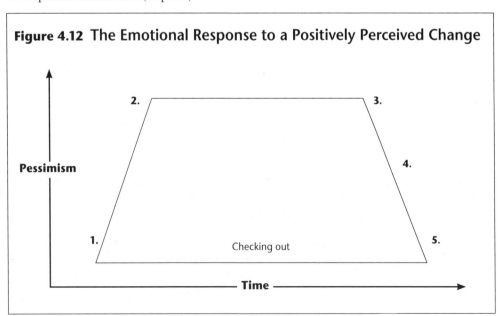

Figure 4.12 The Emotional Response to a Positively Perceived Change

4. Informed optimistic state (confident)
5. Real state (satisfied)

During the uninformed optimistic state, the target feels very positive about the proposed change and looks forward to the change. The change agent should like the employee's enthusiasm about the project in this state, but should present the individual a practical view of what the project is designed to accomplish.

The positive response cycle has one bailout point—at state 2, the uninformed pessimistic state. At this point, an individual begins to doubt that the change is necessary, that it's beneficial to him or her, and that it's going to produce the desired results. And so the person takes a negative position on the change, not because the change is bad, but because he or she is uninformed about the details of the change. As a result, the person bails out. He or she can bail out publicly, telling management and everyone else that the change is no good and won't work. The public bail out allows management the chance to reason with the employee and explain why the change is necessary. However, employees often bail out privately, talking to their friends and other employees about how bad the future state will be. It can be an undermining force if your employees develop a fifth column whose sole objective is to prove that the change is bad for the organization.

During this stage, the change agent should understand that the employee will have reservations about the project. As a result, the change agent and the target's sponsor should be supportive of the employee, providing a better understanding of the change and its impact on him or her. The change agent and the sponsor should ensure that the employee has enough understanding about the outcome of the project that he or she won't withdraw from it either privately or publicly. If the condition becomes widespread, the change agent should develop a problem-solving climate to resolve the employees' issues.

During the hopeful realism state, the employee begins to see the project as doable. This helps to reduce the negative feeling the employee had about the project. The person begins to gain self-confidence that he or she will be able to handle the change. During this stage, the change agent should continue to develop the target's personal confidence. The change agent should provide a realistic picture of the future-state process so that the employee's expectations are more in line with the projected outcomes. Involving the target in preparing new work instructions also helps.

During the informed optimistic state, as the project become better defined, the employee's negative feelings about the project give way to confidence. The employee has a lot of positive energy and increased self-confidence as the future-state solution begins to take shape. The change agent, during this stage, uses this positive energy to help bring along other targets. Now the change agent communicates the importance of good follow-through for the project to be successful. Getting employees who've reached this state to talk to people who aren't as far along in the cycle helps boost the acceptance of the project.

The last state is the real state (satisfied state). In a well-run project, this is the ongoing state until another change affects the process. In this state, the targets strongly support the change and are willing to help others accept the process. They believe they've gained control over their assignment. Targets are rewarded for completing the positive response cycle. Change agents will follow the activities for a period to be sure no later problems arise and management rewards them for their achievements.

Let me give you a personal example. My organization decided to move my office from the center of the building down to the corner of the building. The new office had windows on two sides, and because I work much more efficiently in natural light, windows are important to me. In an uninformed optimistic state, I was excited about the move and rushed home to tell my wife that I was getting a much bigger and nicer office. She asked me which side of the building the new office was on. I said the south side. She quickly pointed out that the sun could make that a very hot office in the summer. I moved into the uninformed pessimistic state. For the next three days I went down to the new office and felt the windows a number of times, eventually deciding that I didn't want to move. I informed my industrial engineers that I wasn't interested in moving to the new office, but they explained that the paperwork had already been processed and someone else was scheduled to move into my old office. There was nothing they could do about it. However, they agreed that they would move me into another office as soon as one was available. When I moved in I was delighted to find out that there was an air-conditioning thermostat in the office that controlled the temperature, so it never got too hot or too cold. In the end, I refused to move when another office became available because the new office exactly fit my needs.

The negative emotional change cycle consists of eight states. They are:
1. Stability
2. Immobilization
3. Denial
4. Anger
5. Bargaining
6. Desperation
7. Testing
8. Acceptance

This is sometimes called the grief cycle because it's exactly the same cycle you go through when someone you care for dies. You can see that you have to manage a number of bail-out points during these eight states. Unfortunately, most managers and employees don't understand the emotional cycles that accompany organizational change, and as a result, they don't know how to handle the bail-out points, causing a great deal of disruption within the organization.

BUILDING COMMITMENT

Building commitment within all of the projects' stakeholders is essential, but few project managers seem to understand how important it is or know how to do it. They also don't know how easily it can be eroded. The commitment process is made up of three phases.

1. Preparation
2. Acceptance
3. Commitment

Figure 4.13 Commitment Model

Phase I: Preparation
Stage 1: Contact
Stage 2: Awareness

Phase II: Acceptance
Stage 3: Understanding
Stage 4: Positive perception

Phase III: Commitment
Stage 5: Installation
Stage 6: Adoption
Stage 7: Institutionalization
Stage 8: Internalization

Each of these three phases represents a critical juncture in the commitment process. Each phase has several degrees of support (stages) for the change project. (See figure 4.13.)

As an individual or organization moves from one stage to the next, the commitment to the change increases. Also, the degree of effort and time required to invest in the change management process increases based upon the degree of commitment required to support the change project. Figure 4.14 depicts the pluses and minuses for each stage in the commitment model.

When carrying out major organizational change, you can choose from a continuum of change management strategies depending on the change and the degree of acceptance

Figure 4.14 Stages in the Commitment Model: Pluses and Minuses

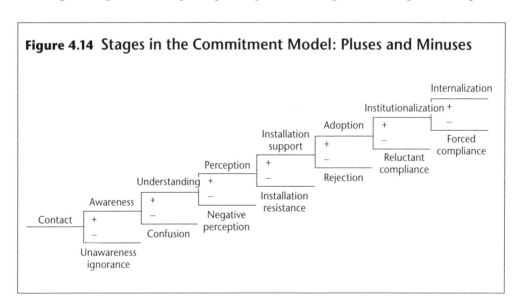

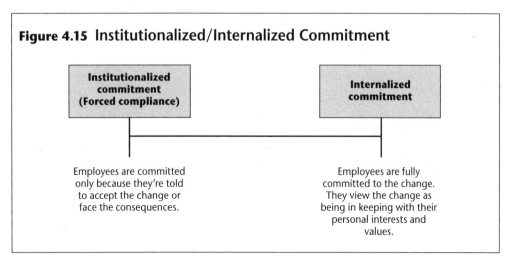

Figure 4.15 Institutionalized/Internalized Commitment

Institutionalized commitment (Forced compliance)

Internalized commitment

Employees are committed only because they're told to accept the change or face the consequences.

Employees are fully committed to the change. They view the change as being in keeping with their personal interests and values.

that the targets must have for it. At one end of the commitment level is "internalized commitment" and at the other end is "institutionalized commitment," which is forced compliance.

Institutionalized Commitment

Not every change requires the people who it affects to believe in it. They may only be required to comply with the change. The targets may accept the changes that are forced upon them because they wish to comply with the organization's activities. The organization motivates the targets to comply by rewarding those who do and punishing those who don't. Targets often mimic acceptable behaviors and learn to do and say what they consider acceptable to the organization. Of course, this approach doesn't have a positive impact on the targets' attitude toward the change. In today's fast-changing environment, most organizations realize that their employees need to understand and support the change. With institutionalized commitment the return on investment is often greatly reduced.

Internalized Commitment

Internalized commitment occurs when the targets believe that the change reflects their personal beliefs, needs, and wants as well as those of the organization. At this level of commitment, the targets take ownership for the success of the change because it satisfies their own needs and because they believe it's good for the organization. At the personal level the change is more embraced and supported than the organization could ever mandate.

RESILIENCY

One key to survival in today's rapidly changing environment is to develop a resilient organization. Resiliency isn't invented. It's liberated.

> "Change is not something that just happens. The CEO and his or her key people have to make the case for change and innovation and they have to create an environment that fosters it."
> —Charles F. Kalmbach
> President and CEO, DBM

Definition: Resiliency is the ability to absorb high levels of disruptive change while displaying minimum dysfunctional behavior.

The resiliency of the project team and of those who are affected by the change (change targets) is an important factor in increasing an organization's ability to absorb change. The more resilient the organization is, the greater its speed of change. A resilient organization has five characteristics:

■ *Positive.* Resilient people display a sense of security and self-assurance that's based upon their view of life as complex but filled with opportunity. Positive individuals or groups:
  ☐ Look for the good, not the bad
  ☐ Look forward to a better future
  ☐ Have a high level of self-esteem
  ☐ Believe they can influence what's going to happen
  ☐ Have a can-do attitude
  ☐ Are energetic

■ *Focused.* Resilient people have a clear vision of what they want to achieve. Focused individuals or groups:
  ☐ Know what they want
  ☐ Prioritize their efforts based upon impact
  ☐ Align personal and organizational goals

■ *Flexible.* Resilient people demonstrate a special ability in thinking and in working with others when responding to change. Flexible individuals or groups:
  ☐ Bend with the wind
  ☐ Can adjust to change
  ☐ Can see things from different perspectives
  ☐ Are open-minded
  ☐ Are open to other people's ideas
  ☐ Like to be a member of a team

- *Organized.* Resilient people are able to develop and find order in ambiguity. Organized individuals or groups:
  - ☐ Like structure
  - ☐ Group information effectively
  - ☐ Plan their activities
  - ☐ Aren't impulsive

- *Proactive.* Resilient people encourage change, rather than defend against it. Proactive individuals or groups:
  - ☐ Have many new ideas
  - ☐ Take risks
  - ☐ Like to see things moving along
  - ☐ Question the status quo

We liken the resilient person to a capacitor and the resistant person to a resistor. In an electronic circuit the resistor just sits there burning energy, but the capacitor stores energy so that it can be used when needed.

The resilient person can reduce the amount of disruption (peak assimilation) of the individual changes by as much as 50 percent while reducing the change impact duration by as much as 25 percent (reducing the time it takes to accept the change). This provides the organization a very competitive advantage.

Resiliency isn't a tool or a methodology; it's an attitude, a culture, the way we behave, and our beliefs. No organization can transform itself into a resilient organization overnight. It takes time to bring about the transformation. The process of raising an individual's original level of resiliency through training, coaching, and rewards is called "raising baseline resiliency to an enhanced level." As the base resilience levels of the individuals who make up the organization move to the enhanced level, the organization's cultures and behaviors will change to reflect the new level of resiliency.

Organizations can measure the level of resiliency enhancement by monitoring the organization's changes in behavior as defined by the five characteristics of resiliency—positive, focused, flexible, organized, and proactive.

It's our experience that when a group of resilient people is affected by change, a great deal of synergy occurs.

Resilient employees live with the same change challenges that everyone else does, but they usually possess the following traits:

- They're physically and emotionally healthier.
- They rebound from the change faster and with less stress.
- They achieve more of the objectives.
- They're more productive.

- They have a higher level of implementation capacity.
- They develop a resilient culture.

"Winners look at change as buildings blocks. Those who fight change find themselves serving as the foundation that someone else builds upon."

—HJH

THE EIGHT CHANGE RISK FACTORS

Eight risk factors have to be managed during any major change initiative. They are:

- Defining the cost of the status quo
- Developing a clear vision
- Obtaining sponsored commitment
- Developing change agents and change advocacy skills
- Understanding targeted responses
- Aligning the change with the culture of the organization
- Anticipating internal and external organizational events
- Developing sound implementation architecture

A 2001 Gartner Group report estimated that inexperience, overextension, or under-committed executive sponsorship would account for 50 percent of change-initiative failures. Less than 35 percent of change-management initiatives will include custom strategies for managing change resisters or taking best advantage of early change adapters, thereby unnecessarily constraining the organization's overall capacity. It also states that 75 percent of change leaders will employ one or more levers to help drive change without possessing even a rudimentary understanding of the implications, directly causing destructive organizational behaviors.

> **"Unfortunately, many organizations go for buy-in on new processes or systems after they introduced it, and the results can be catastrophic."**
> **—Robert Kriegel**
> **Author, *If it Ain't Broke . . . Break it!***

WHAT PROJECTS NEED CHANGE MANAGEMENT?

Organizational change management isn't a stand-alone project. It usually supports some other project. It shouldn't be applied to all projects as some projects are low risk and will progress well without the additional change efforts. OCM should be applied to projects that have any of the following characteristics:

- All major project changes
- Projects with a high cost as a result of failure

- Projects with a high risk that human factors could result in failure
- Projects with an unusually short project cycle

All the information contained in this chapter should be applied to all projects that meet any one of these conditions.

THE SEVEN PHASES OF THE CHANGE MANAGEMENT METHODOLOGY

"Change management approaches may sound like common sense but, too often, common sense is not commonly practiced."

—HJH

To offset the many problems that occur if the affected employees aren't made a part of the project before it's put into place, a seven-phase change management methodology has been developed that starts as soon as the project team is assigned. (See figure 4.16.) Following are more details related to each of the seven phases.

Phase I—Clarify the Project

In phase I the project team defines the scope of the project and the level of commitment by management and the affected employees that's required for the project to succeed.

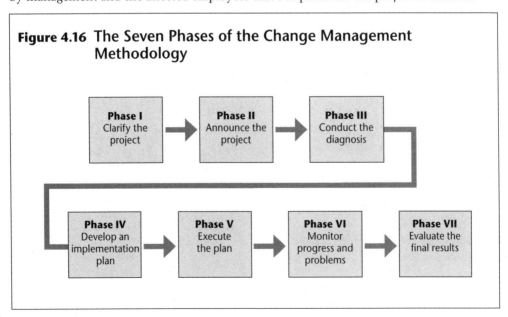

Figure 4.16 The Seven Phases of the Change Management Methodology

Phase II—Announce the Project

In phase II the team develops a tailored change management plan and communicates it to all the affected constituents. Careful planning and sensitivity to the unique needs of various groups will minimize disruption and set the stage for acceptance of the need for the change.

Phase III—Conduct the Diagnosis

During phase III the team uses surveys and other types of analysis tools (e.g., landscape survey) to determine any barriers that could jeopardize the success of the change. This diagnostic data, coupled with the rich dialogue that occurs during phase II, provides the basis for developing an effective implementation plan.

Phase IV—Develop an Implementation Plan

The implementation plan defines the activities required to successfully carry out the project on time, within budget, and at an acceptable quality level. Typical things that will be addressed in this plan are:

- Implications of status quo
- Implications of desired future state
- Description of the change
- Outcome measures
- Burning-platform criteria
- Comprehensive or select application of implementation architecture
- Disruption to the organization
- Barriers to implementation
- Primary sponsors, change agents, change targets, and advocates
- Tailoring of announcement for each constituency
- Approach to pain-management strategies
- Actions to disconfirm status quo
- Alignment of rhetoric and consequence management structure
- Management of transition state
- Level of commitment needed from which people
- Alignment of project and culture
- Strategies to improve synergy
- Training for key people
- Tactical action steps
- Major activities
- Sequence of events

Phase V—Execute the Plan

The goal of phase V is to fully achieve the human and technical objectives of the change project on time and within schedule. It's designed to achieve these objectives by reducing resistance and increasing commitment to the project.

Phase VI—Monitor Progress and Problems

The goal of phase VI is to keep the project on track by consistently monitoring results against the plan.

Phase VII—Evaluate the Final Results

The intent of phase VII is to provide a systematic and objective collection of data to determine if the tangible and intangible objectives of the project have been achieved and to provide insight into lessons learned and potential problem areas that may arise in future change projects.

CHANGE MANAGEMENT TOOLS

Change management includes almost fifty unique change management tools. Some of them are:

- Cultural assessment
- Landscape surveys
- Change agent evaluation
- Change history survey
- Change resistance scale
- Overload index
- Predicting the impact of change
- Role map application tool
- When to apply implementation architecture

Figure 4.17 indicates where these tools can be used in each of the seven phases of the change management methodology. The book *Project Change Management* (McGraw-Hill, 2000) by Daryl R. Conner, Nicholas L. Horney, and myself, provides detailed information on each of these fifty change management tools. The surveys and evaluations that make up the change management tools were developed by Daryl R. Conner and his team at ODR, which is now called Conner Partners. (You can buy these tools by contacting Conner Partners, 1230 Peachtree Street, Suite 1000, Atlanta, GA 30309, (404) 564-4800, *www .connerpartners.com.*)

Figure 4.17 OCM Assessments, Planning Tools, and Training

OCM Assessments (A), Planning Tools (P), and Training (T)	Pre-work¹	I	II	III	IV	V	VI	VII
Change agent evaluation (A)	X			X				
Change agent selection form (A)	X			X				
Change history survey (A)		X						
Change project description form (P)	X	X	X	X	X	X	X	X
Change resistance scale (A)				X				
Communicating change project analysis (P)			X					
Communicating change constituency analysis (P)			X					
Communicating change statement development (P)			X					
Communicating change announcement plan (P)				X				
Culture assessment (A)				X				
Culture audit (A)	X	X	X	X	X	X	X	X
Expectations for a successful change project (A)		X						
Implementation plan advocacy kit (P)					X			
Implementation plan evaluation (A)					X			
Implementation problems assessment (A)				X				
Landscape survey (A)*		X		X		X	X	X
OCM training for sponsors, agents, targets, and advocates (T)	X	X			X			
Organizational change implementation plan (P)					X	X	X	X
Overload index (A)		X				X		
Pain management strategies sponsor (P)	X							
Postmortem process**								X
Predicting the impact of change (A)		X		X				
Preliminary implementation plan (P)					X			
Role map application tool (P)	X	X	X	X	X	X	X	X
Senior team value for discipline (A)		X						
Sponsor checklist (A)		X		X				
Sponsor evaluation (A)		X		X				
Synergy survey (A)		X		X				
When to apply implementation architecture (A)		X						

¹ Pre-work — Used before starting Phase 1   * This assessment tool is scored by ODR's Diagnostic Services

** This project-effectiveness evaluation tool isn't OCM specific

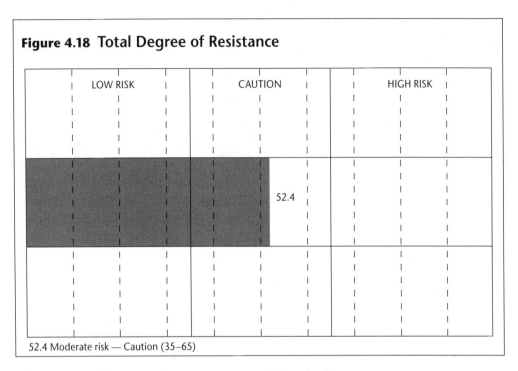

Figure 4.18 Total Degree of Resistance

| LOW RISK | CAUTION | HIGH RISK |

52.4

52.4 Moderate risk — Caution (35–65)

Change-Resistance Assessment and Analysis

So that you better understand how the fifty change management tools are used, we're providing a real example of how one was used. This is an example of a change resistance analysis that reflects the perceptions of sales, business operations, and external service organizations about a specific process redesign project. Figure 4.18 shows the total degree of resistance.

A resistance factor in this range is high enough that it should be considered a significant issue in predicting the success or failure of putting the change into place. Target resistance will be a pivotal element in the project's outcome and therefore requires attention and resources in the planning and implementation steps. Figure 4.19 shows the resistance by individual assessment items.

An analysis of the individual items for customer service revealed the following enablers and barriers to the change. Any item scored in the range of low-risk opportunity indicates a low level of resistance and a positive prognosis for project success. The analysis also revealed a number of significant barriers to change that scored over 6.5 and that warrant careful consideration. Any item that scored in this range indicates a high level of resistance and a negative prognosis for success. However, any score over 3.5 places the item in the danger zone and shouldn't be ignored. Here's a list of the perceived enablers or barriers of the change.

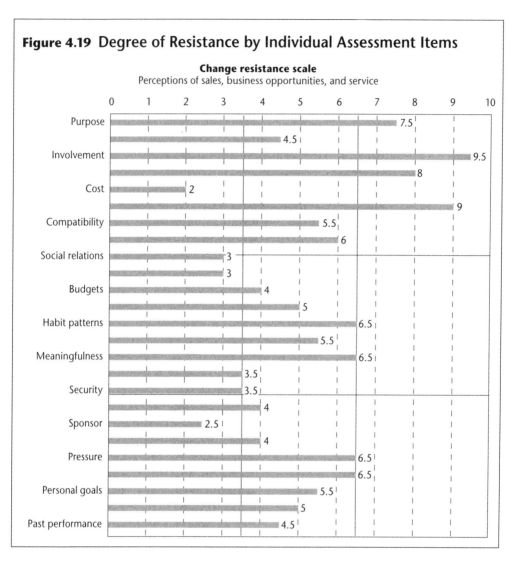

Figure 4.19 Degree of Resistance by Individual Assessment Items

Change resistance scale
Perceptions of sales, business opportunities, and service

- Enablers
    - [ ] (5) Cost (score 2.0): The degree to which targets think that the change has a physical, intellectual, or emotional cost.
    - [ ] (19) Sponsor (score 2.5): The degree to which targets have a high level of trust and respect for the sponsor.
    - [ ] (9) Social Relations (score 3.0): The degree to which targets perceive that relationships that are important will be improved or remain positive because of this change.
    - [ ] (10) Support (score 3.0): The degree to which targets believe that organizational resources will be provided for this change.

- Barriers
  - ☐ (3) Involvement (score 9.5): The degree to which the targets believe they've had input into the planning of this change.
  - ☐ (6) Reward (score 9.0): The degree to which targets think that there are adequate rewards for accomplishing the change.
  - ☐ (4) Communication (score 8.0): The degree to which targets think communication about the change has been made clear.
  - ☐ Purpose (score 7.5): The degree to which the targets believe the purpose of the change is clear.

For each of the barriers (high-risk items), you must prepare mitigation plans. In the example, mitigation plans were prepared for all items that had a rating of 6.0 or greater (nine mitigation plans).

SUMMARY

The OCM methodology isn't designed to help the organization define what change decisions to make. What it does do is help define how to best carry out the decisions in a way that reduces the risks of failure and generates the support required for project success. It contains an approach that allows sophisticated concepts to be addressed in a very practical way. It provides ways to measure risk and barriers and approaches to decreasing their impact on the organization.

Note: Much of the input for this chapter came from the book *Project Change Management* (McGraw-Hill, 2000) by Daryl R. Conner, Nicholas L. Horney, and myself. Much of the content was based upon work done by ODR. The OCM assessment, planning tools, and training tools are the exact names of ODR products. ODR has since been renamed Conner Partners.

CHAPTER V

REINFORCING DESIRED BEHAVIOR

"Why is it we train managers how to handle unsatisfactory employees but not how to thank the ones who perform?"
—HJH

The saying goes, "Put your money where your mouth is." There's more truth than fiction in this statement. If you want people to change, show your appreciation when they try to or do change. You should watch for the slightest change in behavior and make sure the person knows you recognize the effort it required, and it always takes effort to change. I once worked with a man who always showed up late—twenty-five to thirty minutes. We started work at 8 a.m. and he would walk in at 8:30, always with another excuse. He didn't have an alarm clock so I personally called him to wake him up, and even that didn't work. One day he came in at 8:15 and I complimented him. Each time he got in earlier I went out of my way to show him I realized he was trying. Before long he was the one who got to work early enough to make the coffee for the rest of us.

> "Populist leaders encourage people to develop their own form of teamwork and their personal ownership of competitive improvements."
> —Armand V. Feigenbaum

The rewards and recognition system plays a key role in any change management process. Basically, we're trying to change the behavioral patterns of management and the employees. To accomplish this, we must change our rewards and recognition system. If you make no change to the rewards and recognition system, you can't expect any long-term change in the organization's behavioral patterns. Figure 5.1 is a change process chart. The different levels of change are:

> "The greatest need of every human being is the need for appreciation."
> —William James
> Harvard psychologist

- P1—This is the present performance level of the organization. You'll note a lot of variation in the performance level and a big difference between good and bad performance.
- P2—This is the preferred performance level of the organization. It's at a much higher performance level with a lot less variation.
- P3—This is the pain level. If performance drops below this level, management takes action to correct the problem. This action can take many forms, from no pay increases to being fired.

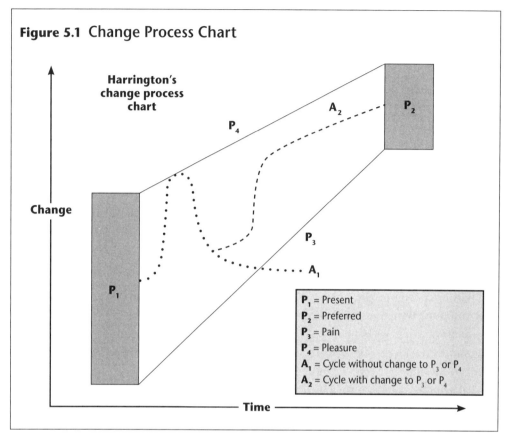

Figure 5.1 Change Process Chart

- P4—This is the pleasure level. It's the performance level where the individual or group receives special recognition for a job well done. It can take on the form of bonuses, promotions, salary increases, extra vacation, new offices, etc.
- A1—This is the cycle that performance goes through as a result of change initiatives if there's no change in the pleasure and pain system. You'll note that when the new process stabilizes, the performance level increases to a point and then drops back to its existing level.
- A2—This shows the performance level when the pleasure and pain system is changed to reflect the desired behavioral patterns.

You'll note that some of the behavioral patterns that are being punished are the same ones that previously were considered reward-warranted behaviors.

"Praise loudly and blame softly."
—HJH

REWARDS AND RECOGNITION SYSTEM

If you change the process and want to change individual behavior patterns, you need to change the way you reward and recognize your staff. If you reward people in the same old way, they'll behave in the same old way. That's why the organizational change management (OCM) methodology includes rewards and recognition as a key element. The changes that go on in an organization today are so great that often the behaviors we once rewarded our people for are now considered unacceptable; we may even punish an individual if he or she continues the behaviors. For example, you may once have rewarded an individual for correcting a problem the team created, and now you punish the person because he or she didn't prevent the problem from occurring. Or you may have rewarded a person who was working at the three sigma level (99.8 percent good) and now expect the person to work at the six sigma level (3.4 errors per million opportunities).

> "Successful adults are unlikely to change something unless they are under enormous pressure or have the tools and reinforcement to change."
> —Steven S. Reinemund
> CEO, PepsiCo Inc.

That's enough about poor performers. Let's turn our attention to the other side of the model—the rewards and recognition system. The rewards and recognition system is the pleasure part of the model. You must update it to reflect the new desired behavior patterns brought about by the change processes. All people need recognition; it's a basic human requirement. Your salary is recognition of what your time is worth to the organization. A baby cries to get attention—to be recognized. People striving to be recognized drive the whole competitive society we live in. Recognition is simply having someone else acknowledge your worth. It's something that everyone wants, needs, and strives to obtain. Studies have shown that people classify recognition as one of the things they value most.

EXCERPT: MAKING TEAMS HUM

The following is an excerpt from *Making Teams Hum* (Paton Press, 2006), by Mitch Manning and myself.

Recognition and rewards are essential tools and techniques for making teams hum. The ideal purpose of recognition and rewards is to direct and reinforce positive behavior to achieve the goals of the team. Positive behavior is best reinforced with immediate gratification. Positive results are best reinforced when celebrated immediately after achieving the goal. Therefore, simple and fast recognition and rewards are better than complex and bureaucratic recognition and rewards. Behavior- and results-focused recognition and rewards require planning and structure. Focused, planned, and structured recognition and rewards are equally as important to achieving and sustaining a humming team as any other leadership tool or technique.

The objective is to provide guidelines for focusing, planning, and structuring recognition and rewards to increase team effectiveness and individual performance. The first guideline is to value the organization over the team and the team over the team member. To do otherwise upsets the balance of the organization and defeats the purpose of the team. Organizations are designed to serve people. Unbalanced recognition and rewards defeat the purpose of the organization. The defeated organization can't serve the team(s) and team members. Focusing and structuring recognition and rewards begins with balancing the needs of the team members, the team, and the organization.

The second guideline is that balanced recognition and rewards must honor and respect the will and the spirit of the people. There are three levels to address. First, member rewards and recognition are needed which increase the sense of dignity and self-esteem of each member. Second, the team needs recognition and rewards to increase the team cohesiveness and team spirit. Third, the organization needs rewards and recognition to increase productivity and achievement of goals to sustain and nurture the organization.

Four fundamentals for achieving a high performance organization were referenced in Edward E. Lawler, Susan Albers Mohrman, and Gerald E. Ledford's book, *Strategies for High Performance Organizations* (Jossey-Bass, 1998*)*. The fundamentals of a high-performance organization (humming team) were identified as information, knowledge, power, and rewards. The following is a paraphrase of the authors' conclusions focused on recognition and rewards for making teams hum.

- Without recognition and rewards for team performance, things like information, knowledge, and power are dangerous. Nothing will ensure that team members will exercise their information, knowledge, and power in ways that will contribute to team effectiveness.
- Recognition and rewards for organizational performance without power, information, and knowledge lead to frustration and lack of motivation because people can't influence their recognition and rewards.

- Without focused, planned, and structured recognition and rewards, information, knowledge, and power are likely to lead to poor individual, team, and organization decisions.
- Recognition and rewards, information, and knowledge without power lead to frustration because people can't use their expertise to discipline their behavior to achieve the desired results.

Real Story

The power of simple, fast, focused, and structured recognition and rewards to influence behavior and achieve results is illustrated by this true story. It's about a team self-named the Shifters. The story is an amazing example of the power of team involvement and ownership of recognition and rewards to quickly and effectively change behavior and achieve targeted results. It would be good to stop with the accomplishment, but that wouldn't be the whole story. The whole story includes a disappointing end. The end is included to be used as a learning point for the pitfalls of "the best intentions" of recognition and rewards.

The Shifters worked third shift in the special packaging division of MegaCorp. In less than four months the Shifters went from last place to first place in production efficiency in the division. This would've been surprising if all shifts were equal in staffing knowledge, training, and experience. Considering the differences in these areas between the first- and second-shift employees and the Shifters, the climb to the top was astounding.

The Shifters were made up of the newest hires and the weakest performers in the division. When their production efficiencies started to climb from 85 percent efficiency into the low 90s, eyebrows were raised. When their numbers climbed above 100 percent, investigations were started. The first "discovery" was a converted bulletin board in a hallway leading to the Shifters work area. It seems that someone had turned it into a scoreboard of sorts. The board was covered neatly in rows of batch numbers. Each batch number had either a *w* or an *l* beside the date. New batch numbers with letters appeared daily. At the earliest dates there were many *l*'s. The most recent dates and batches were nearly all *w*'s. When questioned, the Shifters proudly proclaimed that the *w*'s were wins and the *l*'s were losses. Whenever the Shifters met or exceeded the standard production efficiency they recorded a *w* for a win. Just weeks into the process they had practically eliminated all *l*'s (losses) from their scoreboard.

The in-depth investigation didn't start until the Shifters started to routinely post 135 percent production efficiency. This happened in less than four months. Members of the day shift's management team started to drop in on the third shift to "just see how things were going." It wasn't long before the Shifters were found out. It was around mid-shift (3 a.m.) during the third month that a first-shift supervisor observed the Shifters having a celebratory pizza party in the cafeteria. They were celebrating completing the previous week above 100 percent production efficiency and that two members had completed cross training in all jobs in the area. The cross-trained members were actually awarded a certificate by their co-workers. The certificate proudly pronounced the bearer as a Ph.D. in special packaging cross training.

Before the end of the fifth month the pizza parties were eliminated, the certificates were banned, the scoreboard was taken down, and the group leader was moved to day shift. Almost immediately, the production efficiency on third shift started a downward slide. Before the year was over production efficiency was back at 85 percent. The slide was not without pain for the members, the team, the division, and MegaCorp. Even now members of the Shifters and their former group leader voice bitterness about the big bust-up. They still can't understand why members of the other shifts complained about the cross training that the Shifters received, the pizza parties that they paid for with their own money, and the certificates that they awarded to members who completed cross-training. They don't understand why the group leader was punished for getting them involved in improving the production efficiency. The only answer they ever got was, "That's not how things are done around here."

Hopefully, you're experiencing disbelief and have questions that need answers. Using your own experiences and the information already provided in this chapter, answer the following questions. Why do you think the Shifters improved so quickly? Why do you think the day shift management team wasn't supportive? What would you have done differently, if you were the group leader of the Shifters?

Could it be that the recognition and rewards captured the will and the spirit of each Shifter? What's the difference between recognition and reward? What's will and spirit? What's the importance of will and spirit to directing and reinforcing positive behavior to achieve goals? Is it possible that simpler, faster, and better recognition and rewards can be identified, designed, and implemented by the members of the team? Is it possible that excellence can be rejected if the explanation is so simple everybody could do it? Is "We did it because we wanted to do it" really incomprehensible? Take time to write your answers before continuing to read.

Reward: Something such as money, given or offered especially for a special service such as the return of a lost article or the capture of a criminal. A satisfying return or a result. To give a reward. To satisfy or gratify; recompense.

Recognition: The act of recognizing or condition of being recognized. Attention or favorable notice. To show acknowledgment or approval.

Will: The mental faculty by which one deliberately chooses or decides upon a course of action; volition.

Spirit: The essential nature of a person. The part of a human being associated with the mind and feelings as distinguished from the physical body. The fundamental character or disposition of an individual; temperament.

So far we've given two guidelines for simpler, faster, and better team recognition and rewards. Now, it's time to complete the guidelines. They are:

- Value the organization over the team and the team over the team member.
- Honor (value) the will and the spirit of the people.
- Value behavior over results.
- Value results over consequences (recognition and rewards).
- Value subjective and objective.
- Value equity over parity.
- Value recognition over rewards.
- Recognize and reward what you value. (Say what you'll do. Do what you say.)

The guidelines are based on a situation-specific model of human performance.

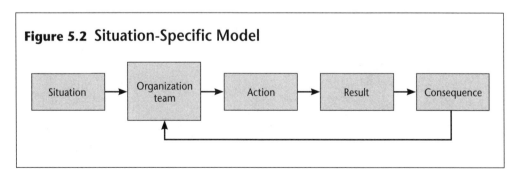

Figure 5.2 Situation-Specific Model

Situation → Organization team → Action → Result → Consequence

Behavior: The actions or reactions of persons or things under specified circumstances (situation).

Results: The consequence of a particular action, operation, or course.

Equity: The state, ideal, or quality of being just, impartial, and fair.

Parity: Equality, as in amount, status, or value.

Objective: Impersonal. Uninfluenced by emotion, surmise, or personal prejudice.

Subjective: Personal. Existing only in the mind. Influenced by emotion, surmise, or personal prejudice.

The two principles of team recognition and rewards are now self-evident. They are:

- Recognition and rewards for making teams hum are value-based and value-added.
- Recognition and rewards for making teams hum are behaviorally focused and result-driven.

The power of these principles has been demonstrated time after time in every facet of my life from childhood to the present. I believe it's because they're directly aligned with the natural law, "You reap what you sow." In a very special way, team recognition and rewards are our seeds of appreciation. Our approach to "cultivating" team behavior must be focused, planned, and structured. Because the human need to be appreciated is the most fertile field to cultivate when you need to direct and reinforce positive behavior to achieve the goals of the team. My experience has always been that the simpler and faster means of showing appreciation have always worked better. I've seen industry leaders commit their organizational assets to a national cause to receive a pat on the back from the U.S. president. I've seen elementary school children in an impoverished community commit their total assets (themselves and family) to improve and beautify their school for a simple "thank you" from the teachers and staff. These examples are worlds apart, but stand on the same solid foundation of appreciation. We want to share with you a real story that we think exemplifies the concepts and principles covered so far.

Real Story

To set the scene, one author has always lived in the same small community in one of the eleven most economically disadvantaged counties in North Carolina. He learned early in life that if you wanted something to happen that you had to commit to roll up your sleeves and work to make it happen. His parents had no property, very little money, less than eight years of public schooling between the two, and six children. Two children were physically challenged. He learned early from my parents that God (spirituality/connectedness/nature/faith) is first and family is second.

By the time his two children were in elementary school, he was deeply involved in school and community activities. In his late twenties and early thirties, he was president of the Parent Teacher's Association (PTA), member of the local school advisory board, member of the fire and rescue squad, president of the local Lions Club, and coach of the Seaboard Savings and Loan T-ball team. Fortunately for him, he thought that the economic and education situation in his family and community prepared him to be a situational learner early in life. He had learned to learn from every situation.

He learned, or at least reinforced, most of what he believed about team recognition and rewards during a three-year stint as the T-ball coach. Six- to nine-year-olds are great teachers. The parents of six- to nine-year-olds are great critics and give good feedback to their children's coaches. His point was that opportunity for learning in this situation was very, very ripe.

The first year of coaching he had the very best talent in the league. However, the team didn't win the league championship. A big reason was that he was still learning how to play baseball. Needless to say, he was often reminded of the missed opportunity. It was on his mind for the rest of the year.

There's more to the story. You see, his team was 80 percent minority. More than half of them were from single-parent homes. At the first meeting of the second season he was firmly convinced that he owed that team more than they had gotten from him the previous year. He wanted them to think like winners and to feel like winners. He knew he couldn't do it alone. So he asked them on opening day if they wanted to win the league championship. "Yes" came the resounding chorus. He liked what they said, so again and with more energy, he asked, "Do you want to win the championship?" "Yes, Yes" came the thunderous reply. "Are those other teams really any better than us?" he asked. "No." This proud young team bellowed. "Well then, do you like to win?" "Yes," they replied. "What do you get when you win?" he asked. "Pizza," they hungrily resounded.

To be perfectly honest he wasn't ready for that one. He knows now that in the spirit of the situation, he was very vulnerable. He replied, "If you win today, and every time you win this year, we'll go out for pizza." The team was ecstatic! Not knowing what else to say, he paraphrased the coach that had mentored him in the off-season. "Well then, let's play by the rules, play our positions, back up our team mates, always go for the win, and we'll get better every game. We'll eat lots of pizza."

That night as the steaming pizzas were delivered, Jimmy Witherspoon reportedly ate five pieces of pizza before the plates reached the table. About eight or nine pizzas later, Vince Brown, the smallest player on the team, slid into the seat beside his coach. He grabbed his arm and looked him straight in the eye. With pizza sauce all over his face and in both ears, he said, "Mr. Mitchell," this is the best day of my whole life." He looked back and said, "Me too, Vince. Me too." This moment was broken by painful moans coming from a nearby booth.

"Mr. Mitchell," several small, scared voices called. "Jimmy Witherspoon is awfully sick. He thinks he might be dying." Expecting the worst he rushed over to find Jimmy twisted and contorted on the bench. He was moaning, "It hurts, my stomach hurts. It's killing me." The gravity of the situation was obvious. Jimmy, a person of much color, was an unexpected shade of dark green. At least the parts not covered by pizza crust and sauce were dark green. "What is it Jimmy?" he asked. "He tried to eat all of our pizza," the team chorused. "It hurts bad, Mr. Mitchell," moaned Jimmy. But then he drew himself up and in his best manly voice he said, "It does hurt real bad, but I still feel real good everywhere else, Mr. Mitchell."

So, on opening day of the second T-ball season he learned that the members and the team know what it takes to recognize and reward results, winning deserves immediate rewards, and that it's only right to say what you'll do and then to do what you say for recognition and rewards. He also learned that recognition and rewards can feel good and hurt bad at the same time. He realized and understood more completely now that recognition and rewards give us some of the best days of our whole lives. That's the primary reason why team recognition and rewards need to be focused, planned, and structured for making teams hum.

Many summers ago, members of that team finished high school and then some finished college. Some had athletic scholarships and some had academic scholarships. Today, a few members of that team are experiencing more recognition and rewards in their careers than most of us will ever know. And the coach still feels a sense of achievement and appreciation when they succeed. Some still call him "coach." Some parents still call him "coach." The sense of appreciation, the real recognition and rewards, are still coming these many years later. A few members of the team, thankfully a very few, had too few winning days and far too few winning seasons. He was glad for them that they had their time on the field, in the arena, at the pizza parlor, their place in the spotlight, and their days in the sun. Recognition and rewards are the drivers behind making all teams hum and this is why we do it.

He hopes some day to more fully understand how recognition and rewards played such a big part in shaping the lives of these young team members and their families. He has a sense that they were influenced in at least four different ways. The first and most important way is what he's learned to call *connectedness,* or *spirituality*. The coach, members, and team were somehow lifted above reality to a very special playing field. This is a synergistic playing field where the whole is greater than the sum of the parts. The members of this team obviously felt a part of something special. They said it in their own ways and others outside the team commented on it as well. This explains to the coach the first guideline, which is to put the organization above the team and the team above the team member.

The second and most obvious influence is that they were physically involved in the whole process. This explains the guideline to recognize and reward behavior before results. He'd always heard that it's not what you say, but what you do. The team sensed ownership of the physical recognition and reward (pizza), and this somehow tempered their commitment to winning. The third influence was mental. Each team member demonstrated consistently and continuously that they were challenged to think about how to win each game and how to behave after winning. This mental challenge somehow resulted in the development of their decision-making and problem-solving skills and abilities. The fourth influence was emotional. These team members were touched by the appreciation sensed as a result of the recognition and rewards. This explains the guideline to value subjectivity over objectivity. He didn't think that you can direct the will and energize the spirit of any person without touching them emotionally. The will is personal strength and the spirit is personal sensitivity. These two human characteristics are the targets of team recognition and rewards for making teams hum.

This leads us to the question, "What behaviors warrant team recognition and rewards?" He learned that there are only four. They are:

- Playing by the rules (the regulations, procedures, policies). The rules reflect what we value and values shape and direct our behavior (ethics).
- Getting the job done (the products and services). Our products and services guide us to what we must do.
- Looking after the resources (the people, technology, capital, and other natural resources). Our resources give us ownership that is the foundation of our commitment.
- Preparing for the next step (this is developing our knowledge, skills, and abilities for satisfying the customers, following directions, and developing and supporting our resources). The next steps connect us to our vision and ground us to our mission.

"Be assured that the most lasting team recognition and rewards are found during the journey, not at the destination."

—HJH

RECOGNITION

Why does recognition matter? George Blomgren of Blomgren Consulting Services Ltd., puts it this way: "Recognition lets people see themselves in a winning identity role. There is a universal need for recognition and most people are striving for it."

A 1994 National Science Foundation study pointed out, "Of all the factors which help to create highly motivated/highly satisfied workers, the principal one appears to be that effective performance be recognized and rewarded—in whatever terms are meaningful to the individual, be it financial or physical or both."

The truth is that people hear "thank you" in many different ways. One wants a plaque to put on the wall while another wants a little extra spending money. Someone else might prefer a couple days of additional vacation time. For example, Tom would be embarrassed if his manager pointed out that he'd made a major contribution to the department during a department meeting. He'd have been much happier if his manager had stopped by his desk and said "thank you" privately. Mary, on the other hand, would love the public recognition. An effective reward system has to provide management many different ways to say "thank you," so

> **"The solution here lies in designing a motivation and reward system based on these generic characteristics and needs of knowledge workers, simultaneously allowing flexibility and free choices within the reward system."**
> **—Catherine L. Wange and Pervaiz K. Ahmed Management Consultants**

that it can match the reward and recognition to the contribution, the situation, and the individual's needs.

The seven types of recognition are:

■ Financial compensation
■ Monetary awards
■ Personal public recognition
■ Group public recognition
■ Private recognition
■ Peer recognition
■ Organizational awards

Financial Compensation

A 1994 study conducted by the Public Agenda Foundation found that more than 70 percent of employees in the United States think that the reason work effort has deteriorated is because there's no connection between pay and performance. This study indicates that productivity for organizations that use incentive plans is as much as 60 percent higher than for those that don't have a work measurement system. One of W. Edwards Deming's fourteen points is to do away with individual performance measurement systems. I disagree with this; everyone wants to be measured. The only ones who don't are the poor performers. If you don't measure the good performers, they'll find ways to measure themselves, and those ways may not be in line with the organization's goals. Pay-for-performance is a critical part of the change process, but salaries aren't the only type of financial compensation. Other typical types of financial compensation are:

■ Commissions
■ Piecework
■ Stock option plans
■ Cash bonuses
■ Gain sharing

Monetary Awards

The word "award" indicates that it's a unique recognition of an individual or small group for an unusual contribution to the organization's goals. Monetary awards are one-time bonuses paid to the recipient immediately after he or she makes an unusual contribution or one that far exceeds expectations. Individuals may also receive them for long-term, continuous, and high-level performance or unique leadership. Management and fellow workers should perceive a person who receives a monetary award as an individual who has contributed something special. The ten basic categories for receiving monetary awards are:

■ Economic value
■ Managerial excellence

- Engineering or scientific contributions
- New concept activities
- Commercial or industrial achievement
- Demonstration of initiative or resourcefulness
- Exceptional effort
- Patents or disclosures
- Improvement achievement
- Preventive activities

Personal Public Recognition

The only limitation on this type of recognition lies in the creativity of the management team. One organization in New York City had a huge billboard put on top of the plant that flashed the names and accomplishment of special individuals. Typical individual public recognition ideas are:

- Promotion
- Office layout
- Annual recognition at conferences
- Jewelry
- Articles in the company newsletter
- Employee pictures posted in the office
- Verbal recognition at department, division, or organizational meetings
- Special job assignments
- Plaques presented to the individual

> **"What gets recognized, gets done and what gets rewarded, gets repeated."**
> **—William James**
> **Author, psychologist, and philosopher**

Many service organizations select an "employee of the month," whose picture is posted in a prominent location. A typical plaque would read, "Rick Harrington deserves national attention for outstanding performance during May 2005."

Group Public Recognition

Today teams that attack problems or design and carry out projects are the rule rather than the exception. To single out one member of the team to receive rewards or recognition would be wrong. The team, working together, builds synergy that adds much more value than any individual working alone. That's why we must have rewards and recognition approaches that recognize groups of people who work together to accomplish an objective. Typical group public recognition ideas are:

- Group mementos (pen sets, calculators, product models, etc.)
- Articles in the company newsletter
- Family recognition picnics

- Lunches with upper management
- Group's attendance at technical conferences
- An evening party for group members and their significant others

Private Recognition

Few things will improve morale and individual performance more than the manager's expressing his or her sincere thanks for an accomplishment or on a personal occasion.

You should give these "moments of sunshine" freely, sincerely, and frequently. Managers should seek out reasons to say, "Job well done," or to recognize some personal thing that's important to the individual. These private moments usually occur in a very informal environment, such as when the manager stops by the employee's workstation or during a chance meeting at the coffee machine. Typical ways to give personal, private recognition are:

- Send a birthday card to the employee at home.
- Write a personal note on a report that the individual prepared and send it back.
- Stop by the person's desk to thank him or her for working on Saturday.
- Take the person to lunch on the anniversary of the day he or she started work for the organization.
- Send a letter to the employee's home from the manager or upper management with thanks for a specific contribution.
- The performance evaluation that takes place every three months is an ideal time to give private feedback to the employee about accomplishments; it shouldn't be the first time that you've expressed your appreciation, but you should use it to reinforce the favorable work patterns and summarize the employee's accomplishments. The most basic rule of performance evaluation is "no surprises."

Peer Recognition

Few things are more valued by individuals than to have their peers recognize them for their accomplishments. The Oscar that's given out at the annual Academy Awards is cherished for a lifetime. Anyone would give his or her left arm to win a Nobel Prize. No greater honor can be bestowed on an individual than to be recognized by the people who do similar jobs. Today many organizations apply this same concept. When I was at IBM, we had all of the employees in quality assurance select the quality inspector, quality manager, and quality engineer of the year.

Management often turns over annual award events to a team of employees to plan the activities. Our experience is that when the employees plan this type of event, it's usually a lot more fun and the winners are very touched. Typically, when management prepares an award ceremony, it turns out to be a ceremony. When employees plan the same event, it turns out to be a party and the gifts that are presented turn out to be from the heart, rather than from the pocketbook.

Organizational Awards

Individuals want to be proud of the organization that they work in. After all, they spend more time at work than at any other single activity. They want to think that the organization they work for is respected and progressive. They want to believe that the work they do is important and contributes to humankind. An effective way to build pride and respect for an organization is to have the organization receive an outside award for outstanding performance. At IBM the plants that produced similar products competed for an annual performance award. The organization that performed the best won a trophy, which it kept until another organization outperformed it. We all worked hard to win and keep this trophy. At General Motors the individual plants are compared to a standard set of criteria and the best-performing plants are recognized.

Recently a series of organizational improvement and accomplishment awards have been given out nationally and internationally. They're setting benchmarks for other organizations. Some of them are:

■ The Deming Prize—Japan
■ Japanese Quality Control Prize—Japan
■ Malcolm Baldrige National Quality Award—United States
■ President's Federal Government Award—United States
■ European Quality Award—Europe
■ Australian Quality Award—Australia
■ International Asian Pacific Quality Award—Pacific Region
■ Best Hardware Laboratory—IBM

TYPICAL REWARDS AND RECOGNITION PROCEDURES

Here's a list of the rewards and recognition system that was developed by one of the organizations we work with.

■ *Monetary awards.* The monetary awards will vary between $2,000 and $10,000 based upon an assessment of the impact of the achievement on the organization or its beneficiaries. Examples are publishing a book that wins international acclaim; long, sustained, exceptional contributions to the organization; or a significant patent.

■ *Personal public recognition.* A dinner for two is an award that's given on the spot for unusually high desired performance. The organization pays for a night out on the town for the employee and his or her significant other. This award shouldn't be given to more than 40 percent of the people in a department during a year's time.

- *Service award.* A silver lapel pin is given to the employee at the first-year anniversary. At the five-year anniversary, it's a gold lapel pin, and at the tenth-year anniversary, it's a gold lapel pin set with a diamond.
- *The golden quill award.* This award is given to individuals who contribute to the organization's knowledge base and its reputation by publishing papers in conference proceedings or in international magazines. The first time a staff member publishes a paper in an international magazine, the person is presented the quill plaque. For each paper published after the first one, a metal tab will be added to the plaque.
- *The president's award.* The President's Award will be awarded annually at two levels (professional and support staff) for contributions to the improvement of the quality of life within the organization. Employees will submit candidates for the award, which is a scarf or a necktie in the company's colors and logo accompanied by $100.
- *Personal private recognition.* The individual manager will recognize the employee privately for each of the following situations:
  - ☐ Birthday
  - ☐ Anniversary in the organization
  - ☐ Wedding day
  - ☐ The birth of a child
  - ☐ Constant and active participation in the department's work effort
  - ☐ Sustained performance in addressing a specific work situation

- *Group public recognition.* The three levels of award are based upon the magnitude of the contribution that the team made to the organization. The awards can vary from a manager's "thank you" to the team at a team meeting to dinner for the team and significant others with the company president and at which each team member receives a personal gift.
- *Peer awards.* Managers, professionals, and support staff, individually or in groups, can nominate candidates for the award. A written narrative is required to support each nomination. These nominations are turned in to the peer-review panel chairman. The peer-review panel selects a professional and staff member of the month and member of the year. The name, picture, and write-up on the award winner will be published in the in-house newsletter and a framed picture of the winner will be displayed in the lobby. The employee of the year gets five days of additional vacation.
- *Annual recognition day.* The annual recognition day is coordinated by personnel and held at the start of a year. At the meeting, which is held off-site, the organization recognizes its staff for service to the organization. The day is marked by a number of activities, including a lunch hosted by the president. The president reviews the past year's accomplishments, thanking the staff for its efforts and sharing management's vision for the next year. The president then recognizes individuals and teams who have won awards, such as the staff member of the year award.

CHAPTER VI

PHASE 3—MANAGING THE ORGANIZATION'S CHANGE PROCESS

"There is often a chance of failure with change. If top management waited until it could make changes error-free, it would paralyze the organization."

—HJH

We've now discussed phases 1 and 2 of the performance improvement management methodology.

- We've discussed ways to define how the organization needs to change.
- We've discussed how to define what the organization needs to do to change and how to develop a total performance improvement management plan.
- We've also discussed organizational change management methodology.

We're now ready to move to phase 3—managing the organization's change process. Specifically, we'll cover how to manage the impact the change has on the organization so as to minimize resistance to the individual change initiatives and to build up resiliency throughout the organization. This is necessary so that everyone can handle the continuously changing business environment that exists in today's public and private sectors.

The two activities related to phase 3 are:

- Activity 3.8—Execute pre-change implementation actions.
- Activity 3.9—Execute post-change implementation actions.

All too often organizations wait until the change is designed and ready to carry out before they start to prepare the affected employees for the change. It typically occurs like this:

- The manager calls the employees together and announces, "We're installing a new customer relationship management (CRM) system next week. Everyone will be going to school on Tuesday and Wednesday."
- Mary responds, "I can't make it. I'll be on vacation."
- Joe joins in, "I can't make it either; I have two meetings scheduled with key customers."
- Harry comments, "I'd like to come, but who will get out the proposal for GTS Corporation? It's due next Friday."

- The manager answers, "It's important that all of you attend so you can use the new software package that comes online the following week."

After the meeting, a conversation at the coffee machine goes like this:
- Mary says, "Does he expect me to cancel my vacation? My family has reservations for a cruise through the Panama Canal."
- Harry chimes in, "It looks as if I'll have to work Saturday and Sunday. That's really tough since I promised my son I'd take him to the ball game."
- Joe says, "This is just another of those information technology (IT) projects that cost a lot and make more work for us."
- Mary says, "In the last company I worked for we installed a new state-of-the-art CRM system that was supposed to increase sales. It didn't work half of the time and I lost six customers trying to use it. My advice to all of you is don't stop using your present system; you know it works. It will take a little time, but management will realize that this is just another IT blunder."
- Tom says, "Don't worry; I'll go to the training class and get copies of the handouts for all of you. That's all you'll need anyway."

And the CRM project goes downhill from there.

It's the pre-change installation of organizational change management (OCM) activities that makes the difference between success and failure. It's a matter of preventing problems and preparing people for change or running around after the change is put in place, finding problems that the change created and correcting them, if you can. It's like running your car into a tree. You may be able to fix it, but it never runs as well as it did before and it's a lot more costly than steering it around the tree.

ACTIVITY 3.8—EXECUTE THE PRE-CHANGE IMPLEMENTATION ACTIVITIES

Here's a good example of how to avoid future shock. In one bank we worked with, the CEO and COO were committed to converting the executive reporting system to a computer-based system. It was a big change in the input and output systems. As a result, the change was divided into phases. The first phase comprised 10 percent of the total and took eighteen months. It covered the profitability of the different parts of the organization. When everyone adjusted to the new system, the users began to want more information about the profitability of the product lines. This led to the implementation of the total system. The result was that the CEO and COO got what they wanted without overtaxing the rest of the organization with so many changes that it went into future shock.

So that you gain a better understanding of how OCM should be applied to a project, an example of a process redesign project will be used. This project had five phases. (See figure 6.1.)

Figure 6.2 shows how the first four phases of the process redesign methodology compare with the seven phases of the OCM methodology.

The first three phases of the process reengineering methodology coincide directly with the OCM pre-change implementation activities. During these three phases the

> "People need to have the skills to function in this new change, but you also have to deal with the other side of them, which is their attitudes, beliefs, and emotions. Companies are not used to dealing with that. They underestimate the power of conviction, the power of emotion, in the change process."
>
> **—Lance Dublin**
> **President and CEO,**
> **Lance Dublin Consulting**

future-state process design is developed and approved. This total cycle will typically take about twenty weeks: six weeks to define what process to redesign and fourteen weeks to define the best future-state solution. The following table is a detailed work breakdown structure that combines the pre-installation activities of a process redesign and an OCM project.

As this example points out, a major part of an effective OCM methodology takes place during the change design activities and before the change starts to be carried out. This is necessary to break down people's resistance to the change and to prepare them to proactively embrace the change when it occurs.

(continues on page 132)

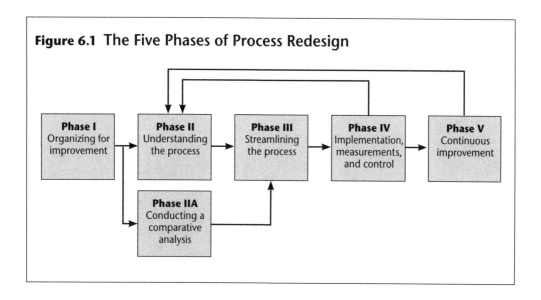

Figure 6.1 The Five Phases of Process Redesign

| **Phase I** Organizing for improvement | **Phase II** Understanding the process | **Phase III** Streamlining the process | **Phase IV** Implementation, measurements, and control | **Phase V** Continuous improvement |

Phase IIA Conducting a comparative analysis

Figure 6.2 The Process Redesign Phases Compared With OCM Phases

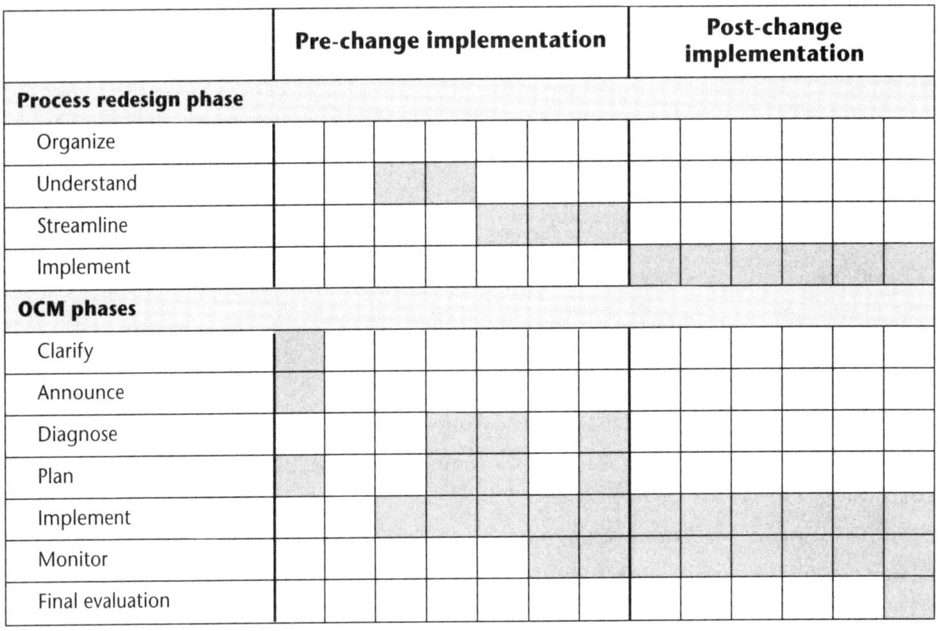

	Pre-change implementation								Post-change implementation					
Process redesign phase														
Organize														
Understand			▒	▒										
Streamline					▒	▒								
Implement									▒	▒	▒	▒	▒	▒
OCM phases														
Clarify	▒													
Announce	▒													
Diagnose			▒	▒		▒								
Plan	▒		▒	▒		▒								
Implement		▒	▒	▒	▒	▒			▒	▒	▒	▒	▒	▒
Monitor					▒	▒			▒	▒	▒	▒	▒	▒
Final evaluation														▒

Figure 6.3 OCM Timeline Chart for a Total Process Redesign Project

No.	Activities and tasks	Weeks									
		–6	–5	–4	–3	–2	–1	1	2	3	4
I	**Organizing for improvement**	▓	▓	▓	▓	▓	▓	▓	▓	▓	▓
1	**Evaluate the applicability of BPI**	▓	▓	▓	▓						
1.1	Prepare the overall business case for BPI (identifying the cost of the status quo and defining the burning platform)	▓									
1.2	Create a future-state vision for the entire project	▓									
1.3	Assess the organization's capacity to assimilate new change using one or more of the following tools as applicable: ■ Change project description form (initial high-level descriptions) ■ When to apply implementation architecture ■ Predicting the impact of change ■ Human due diligence audit ■ Overload index ■ Implementation problems assessment ■ Change history survey		▓								
1.4	Assess the OCM knowledge and skills of the executive team, using one or more of the following tools as applicable: ■ Personal resilience questionnaire ■ Personal power survey ■ Influence style survey ■ Communicating style survey ■ Change knowledge assessment ■ Sponsor evaluation ■ Sponsor checklist ■ Senior team value for discipline		▓								
1.5	Conduct OCM awareness and training as needed to close any gaps found			▓							
1.6	Appoint the BPI champion			▓							
1.7	Assure initiating sponsor and BPI champion of understanding and commitment to OCM			▓							
1.8	Draft and release high-level communications about the BPI project being initiated, the business case requiring it, and the future-state vision.			▓							

(continues)

Figure 6.3 OCM Timeline Chart for a Total Process Redesign Project
(continued)

No.	Activities and tasks	Weeks									
		–6	–5	–4	–3	–2	–1	1	2	3	4
2	**Define critical business procedures**										
2.1	Identify the process and criteria for prioritizing and selecting processes										
2.2	Evaluate such change-relevant factors as: ■ The extent of expected disruption (predicting the impact of change) ■ The change capacity of people involved in the process ■ History of past changes (implementation problems assessment) ■ The subculture of each process (culture assessment) ■ Assess extent and probability of resulting workforce reductions ■ Other changes that would affect people involved in each process										
2.3	Select the critical business processes that will be targeted for BPI										
2.4	Select the BPI methodology that will be applied to each										
2.5	Prioritize the sequence with which BPI will be applied										
2.6	Create a future-state vision for each selected process										
2.7	Set improvement objectives for each selected process										
2.8	Establish a policy and strategy for dealing with workforce reductions										
I	**Organizing for improvement**										
3	**Select the process owners and executive sponsors**										
3.1	Define needed roles and responsibilities										
3.2	Create change role behavior requirements										
3.3	Confirm the role and commitment of the initiating sponsor										
3.4	Evaluate the change capacity and knowledge of potential owners and/or sponsors										
3.5	Select a process owner for each process										

No.	Activities and tasks	Weeks									
		–6	–5	–4	–3	–2	–1	1	2	3	4
3.6	Select an executive sponsor for each process						▓				
3.7	Create project infrastructure (steering committee, project management)						▓				
3.8	Provide OCM training for process owners and sponsors						▓				
4	**Define preliminary boundaries**							▓			
4.1	Define the preliminary scope of each process and/or project							▓			
4.2	Create a preliminary role map diagram							▓			
4.3	Create preliminary communications about the project							▓			
5	**Form and train the process improvement team**							▓	▓		
5.1	Define required team member competencies, skills, resilience, etc.							▓			
5.2	Process-owner block diagram each process to the department level							▓			
5.3	Meet with each affected department manager							▓			
5.4	Select a PIT team member from each affected department							▓			
5.5	Select additional PIT team members as needed (experts, customers, etc.)								▓		
5.6	Select a change facilitator if warranted by the magnitude of the change								▓		
5.7	Create a PIT charter								▓		
5.8	Identify PIT member's existing skills and competencies, etc. using: ■ Sponsor evaluation ■ Change knowledge assessment								▓		
5.9	Create a training plan to close the gap								▓		
5.10	Conduct training and assess results								▓	▓	▓
6	**Box in the process**										▓
6.1	Clarify process and/or project scope—what's included and excluded										▓
6.2	Update the role map diagram based on updated scope information										▓

(continues)

Figure 6.3 OCM Timeline Chart for a Total Process Redesign Project
(continued)

No.	Activities and tasks	Weeks									
		−6	−5	−4	−3	−2	−1	1	2	3	4
6.3	Update the communications plan based on updated scope information										
6.4	Implement the communications plan										
7	**Establish measurements and goals**										
7.1	Determine the metrics to be applied to the process and/or project										
7.2	Establish goals for each metric										
7.3	Create a project-specific change management database										
I	**Organizing for improvement**										
8	**Develop project and change management plans**										
8.1	Create or update the project mission statement										
8.2	Clear statement of the business case (the burning platform)										
8.3	Develop a set of PIT operating guidelines										
8.4	Create individual member assignments										
8.5	Incorporate the process measurements established in activity 7										
8.6	Incorporate the improvement goals for each process metric										
8.7	Identify key barriers										
8.8	Incorporate the current version of the role map diagram										
8.9	Evaluate the extent, causes, and sources of potential resistance										
8.10	Preliminary plan for phases II and III										
8.11	Timetables for completion of phases II and III										
8.12	Identify resource requirements										
8.13	Assess the plan using the OCM implementation plan evaluation										
8.14	Communicate the plan to affected employees										

No.	Activities and tasks	Weeks			
		5	6	7	8
II	**Understanding the process**				
0.1	Ensure commitment and support from sustaining sponsors				
0.2	Provide training for PIT members in phase II tools and skills				
1	**Create process flowchart**				
2	**Prepare the simulation model**				
3	**Conduct process walk-through**				
3.1	Form walk-through teams				
3.2	Conduct a sustaining sponsor commitment analysis				
3.3	Prepare a comprehensive new process vision statement				
34.	Involve sponsors and influencing targets in planning the walk-through				
3.5	Conduct the walk-through				
3.6	Include a culture assessment of the affected areas				
3.7	Define pain associated with the as-is process and potential future state				
3.8	Update the flowcharts and simulation models based on new information				
3.9	Review findings with sustaining sponsors and influencing targets				
4	**Perform process cost and cycle-time analysis**				
5	**Implement quick fixes**				
5.1	Evaluate cost and/or benefit potential				
5.2	Evaluate disruption potential (predicting the impact of change)				
5.3	Select quick fixes to be implemented and develop accelerated plan				
5.4	Secure approval				
5.5	Implement				
5.6	Assess results and impact				
6	**Align process and procedures**				

(continues)

Figure 6.3 OCM Timeline Chart for a Total Process Redesign Project
(continued)

No.	Activities and tasks	Weeks					
		9	10	11	12	13	14
III	**Streamlining the process**						
0.1	Assess the level of sustaining sponsor commitment (sponsor evaluation and/or sponsor checklist) and take needed corrective action						
1	**Apply the 12 streamlining tools to analyze improvement potential**						
1.1	Bureaucracy elimination						
1.2	Value-added assessment						
1.3	Duplication elimination						
1.4	Simplification methods						
1.5	Cycle-time reduction						
1.6	Error-proofing						
1.7	Process upgrading						
1.8	Simple language						
1.9	Standardization						
1.10	Supplier partnerships						
1.11	Automation, mechanization, and information technology						
1.12	Organizational restructuring						
1.13	Interview sponsors and affected people (targets)						
1.14	Prepare new simulation models						
1.15	Prepare a minimum of three alternative future-state solutions						
2	**Perform cost-benefit analysis**						
2.1	Include human costs and benefits						
3	**Select the best-value future-state solution**						
3.1	Use groups of targets to validate solutions						
3.2	Create or update the change project description form						
3.3	Document the business case for selection of the solutions						
4	**Obtain executive committee approval**						
4.1	Reaffirm initiating sponsor commitment to the project						

No.	Activities and tasks	Weeks					
		9	10	11	12	13	14
5	**Approve preliminary implementation plan**						
5.1	Assess the organization's capacity to assimilate the specific change proposed, using one or more of the following tools as applicable: ■ Change project description form (detailed descriptions) ■ When to apply implementation architecture ■ Landscape survey ■ Culture assessment ■ Predicting the impact of change ■ Overload index ■ Implementation problems assessment ■ Change history survey						
5.2	Update the role map document based on best-value solution impacts						
5.3	Assess alignment of the infrastructure with desired behavioral objectives						
5.4	Evaluate the level of teamwork required for successful implementation (synergy survey)						
5.5	Identify infrastructure changes needed to reinforce the change						
5.6	Identify advocates whose help will be needed during implementation						
5.7	Analyze the effectiveness of earlier communications						
5.8	Update the communications plan						
5.9	Identify the training needs of all affected targets						
5.10	Develop a training plan to meet identified needs						
5.11	Identify actual or potential resistance (change resistance scale)						
5.12	Include resistance mitigation activities in the plan						
5.13	Identify actions to be taken by sponsors to maintain target commitment						
5.14	Recommend members of the future-state implementation team (FIT)						

ACTIVITY 3.9 EXECUTE THE POST-CHANGE IMPLEMENTATION ACTIONS

"If you really want to advise me, do it Saturday afternoon between 1 and 4 p.m., and you've got twenty-five seconds to do it, between plays. Not on Monday. I know the right thing to do on Monday."
—Alex Agase
Former Northwestern University football coach

Once the decision is made, nothing will be gained by second-guessing the approach. It's everyone's job to make it happen. It's best to break the change into increments that people can handle, but don't imply that each piece is the end of the change.

You can do a lot to prepare people for the change, but that's like getting dressed to go to a party. The real proof of

Figure 6.4 Change Management Activities During and After Implementation

No.	Activities and tasks	Weeks			
		1 5	1 6	1 7	1 8
IV	**Implementation, measurements, and controls**				
0.1	Assess the level of sustaining sponsor commitment (sponsor evaluation and/or sponsor checklist) and take corrective action where necessary				
0.2	Form the future-state implementation team (FIT)				
0.3	Assess change knowledge of FIT members				
0.4	Assess change agent competence to facilitate phase IV implementation (change agent evaluation)				
0.5	Conduct training as needed in both technical skills and OCM skills				
0.6	Complete a change project description				
1	**Finalize the implementation plan**				
	Review the implementation plan, revise, and update:				
	■ Verify all prior plan activities				
	■ Add any new activities identified by the FIT members				
	■ Detail the plan to the task level				
	■ Assess OCM implications of any changes to the plan				
	■ Identify the individual responsible for each activity and task				
	■ Refine the timetable for completion of each activity and task and assess the cumulative impact of the change timetable				
	■ Update the role map diagram—use it to drive implementation				
	■ Update and implement the communications plan				
	(Organizational change implementation plan and/or implementation plan evaluation)				

how the change will be accepted is when the change is being carried out. Then it will be clear how well it fits into the long-range performance of the organization. As a result, the OCM activities need to continue while the change is carried out and even afterward.

Figure 6.4 continues the phase IV implementation measurements and control phase of the process redesign methodology with the OCM methodology.

Once the change is carried out, the process redesign methodology starts the continuous improvement phase. During this phase, the last phase, phase VII—final evaluation of the OCM methodology, takes place. This is a very important part of the OCM methodology,

No.	Activities and tasks	Weeks			
		15	16	17	18
2	**Implement the new process**				
	Secure the involvement of sponsors, advocates, and target advocates				
	Deliver required training for all targets				
	■ Technical or job skills				
	■ OCM or resilience competencies				
	Implement the planned changes to the infrastructure				
	Communicate the future-state process specifications				
	Provide simulation models of new processes when feasible				
	Implement the planned changes to the process				
	Update simulation models				
	Provide rewards and recognition for adopting new required behaviors				
	Implement plans for removing excess people (sponsors and targets)				
	Maintain frequent contact with sponsors to prevent new "black holes"				
3	**Establish in-process measurements**				
	Include both in-process and outcome measurements				
4	**Establish the feedback systems**				
	Create focus groups to solicit feedback				
	Conduct "town meetings" for collecting feedback				
	Conduct an implementation problems assessment				
5	**Monitor results**				
	Analyze effectiveness of communications				
	Track process measurements against goals				
	Include tracking of human as well as process metrics (landscape survey and/or overload index)				
	Initiate OCM tracking				

for all too often, a new concept is installed but fails to perform to expectations because of technical and/or staff problems. A very critical time occurs just after the change is put in place and the project team that installed the new concept moves on to other challenges. This often creates a void in the support environment in which the affected people (targets) are left to function on their own. The targets can easily become disappointed with the new concept and revert back to their old proven ways of doing things. As a result, the OCM activities should continue for a time after the rest of the project team has been reassigned.

CHALLENGES TO MANAGING THE ORGANIZATION'S CHANGE PROCESS

You must consider many things when an organization decides to implement a change or a new concept. They all present challenges and/or opportunities—they can be enablers or detractors. Whatever they are, they must either be addressed and eliminated or built upon. Sometimes it's hard to tell the good conditions from the bad ones. Some of these are:

- People come in different types.
- Some people just can't or won't perform to the new requirements.
- Change often requires targets to change their behavioral patterns.
- The change does not always fit in with the organization's culture.
- Sometimes old paradigms are hard to give up.

You must consider all of these and many more when you try to manage the organization's change process.

Type-O and Type-D People

"We have to do more—faster and better—with less to survive today. That means we need highly committed people who don't merely put in their time. We need people who are passionate about their jobs and who recommit quickly to creatively redesigning the way they work and communicate. People who are sitting on the change fence need to either buy in or check out."

—HJH

Change produces a crisis when it significantly disrupts our expectations. Chinese writing expresses the concept of crisis with two characters. The top character represents "potential danger"; the lower one conveys "hidden opportunity." Type-D, danger-oriented people, see change as a threat, frequently responding with defensive reaction mechanisms such as denial, distortion, or delusion. Type-O, opportunity-oriented people, while recognizing the dangers and experiencing the same feelings of disorientation, see change as a potential advantage to be explored rather than a problem to be avoided. The extent to which project team members and key leaders have the type-O orientation affects how easily they'll be able to function as effective advocates with their peers. The project manager should evaluate each project team candidate and reject all type-D candidates.

In every project you'll encounter target people who are type-O and type-D. It's very important to identify these people. Most people aren't all one type or another; they're shades between the two. The five words that describe type-O people are:

- Proactive
- Organized
- Positive
- Flexible
- Focused

Think about some of the people you work with or live with and rate them on a scale of 0 to 10, with 0 being a type-O and 10 being a type-D. The type-O people are usually more positive about everything. They:

- See life as fun and rewarding
- Learn from disruption and build a new frame of reference
- Are uncomfortable with change but see it as a new opportunity to take advantage of
- See a glass as half-full, not half-empty
- Like challenges and resist constraints
- Expect disruption because they accept them as part of life
- Don't blame others
- Learn from their mistakes
- Like variation
- Take things as they come and aren't overwhelmed

Unsatisfactory Employees

Much has been written about how to handle employees who are performing unsatisfactorily. It's always a problematic situation to address, and it's unpleasant for both parties. It's much easier for a manager to smile and say, "Joe, you did a good job!" than to have a serious conversation with him about weaknesses in his performance. It's even harder to tell an employee that it's in his or her and the organization's best interests to part ways. Of all the unpleasant tasks I had to perform in the many years I was a manager, the most unpleasant task was firing people—even after having many meetings in which I'd explained why the individual's performance was substandard or because there was no work for that individual. I'd prefer to do just about anything than fire a person.

In the cases in which the organization is changing fast and the acceptable-performance bar constantly moves up, far more than the normal number of employees can perform below standard. These poorly performing employees argue, "At my last performance review, I was rated as an *exceed requirements* performer. Now you're telling me that I don't meet *minimum requirements*. I'm not doing anything different than I was then." That hits the nail on the head. Employees who do the same things the same way year after year are losing ground, and the manager needs to explain that to them. For when you're not improving, you're not just standing still; you're slipping backward because the competition is moving forward.

Some of the many ways to handle poor performers are:

- Counseling
- Reassignment
- Training
- Firing them
- Demoting them
- Ignoring the situation

The worst thing that management can do is to ignore poor performance. When we conduct improvement surveys, the single biggest complaint we get from employees is that management doesn't take action on the "dead wood" within the department. We'd like to think that poor performers would look up to outstanding performers and copy them. What really happens is that the outstanding performers, who are working ten hours a day and some Saturdays to make up for the poor performers, look at the poor performers coming in late and leaving early. They question, "Is the little extra pay worth the extra effort?" As a result, the outstanding performers cut back their work patterns to the standard set by the low performers. This allows the low performers to slip even further and the cycle of performance deterioration takes over.

MANAGING BEHAVIORS DURING IMPLEMENTATION

You'll see in figure 6.5 how big the behavior differences are between organizations that are successful at carrying out change and those that are unsuccessful.

Figure 6.5 **Behavior Differences Between Successful and Unsuccessful Organizations**

Successful Organizations	Unsuccessful Organizations
People are prepared for the change	People are surprised by the change
Targets help put the change in place	Targets get someone else to carry out the change
There is a clear vision of how the change will affect everyone	There is little understanding of the desired results
Projects are selected for OCM	All projects are the same
The project is complete when the change is accepted as the right process	The project is complete when the change is installed
The change output is sustained	The project is complete when the change is installed
Resistance is expected and managed	Resistance is treated as being negative
Ambiguity is tolerated	Ambiguity is not accepted
Management plays a key role in having the change accepted	The project team is responsible for getting the change in place
Employees say, "Let me show you how to make this change work."	Employees say, "I will tell you why this change will not work."
Employees trust management	Employees lose confidence in management because it does not fulfill intentions

CHAPTER VII

CHANGE MANAGEMENT EXCELLENCE SUMMARY

PITFALLS TO SUCCESSFUL OCM

A very good friend, Robert P. Reid, covers fourteen pitfalls to organizational change management (OCM) and their solutions in his lectures. His ideas are worth repeating here.

No Perceived Need for Change

Most individuals and organizations that need change fail to perceive it. Individuals and organizations that are living in denial will accept the status quo until they disappear. A negative situation is what usually causes an individual or organization to perceive the need for change.

No Support From Key Individuals

"Progress is a nice word. But change is its motivator and change has its enemies."
—Robert Kennedy

To be successful, any individual or organization must have support. Support must cover a wide range of time-event horizons, address key interactions, and follow a visible vector. You can't change an organization by yourself. You need a sponsor or mentor who's higher than you in the organization. You must form a coalition of supporters to provide the resources necessary to drive the change.

Pitfall 3—Not Focused on the Correct Goal

Focusing on the correct goal by following the visible vector and making it an integral part of any individual or organization is very difficult to do. Much has been published about how to focus on your long-term outlook, your short-term outlook, maintaining your status quo, and so forth. Each of these is a good focus at the appropriate time based on your context. Setting the goal and not reviewing it frequently in relation to other key factors is a recipe for disaster. Any goal must be frequently reviewed and revised and must not become a meaningless mantra to be repeated and used as an obstacle by organizational sludge.

Lack of Comprehension of Appropriate Time Event Horizon

Failure to understand the need to examine interactions in relation to all of the time event horizons leads to less than optimum success. Lack of understanding of the concept of time event horizons causes individuals and organizations to focus on inappropriate change and is a success inhibitor.

Inability to Change Status Quo

Individuals and organizations tend to follow the law of physics that states, "An object at rest tends to stay at rest." Stagnation is a consistent success killer. Most individuals and organizations don't even realize how stagnant they've become. They believe that because they've come out with a new product, rearranged their physical surroundings, or reorganized their reporting structure that they've made progress. Many find it easier to do nothing or make minor cosmetic changes than to meaningfully address what it takes to influence the major interactions of the status quo. Organizational sludge fights unmercifully to maintain the current bureaucracy and methods.

No Way to Keep Score

Individuals and organizations also tend to follow the law of physics that states, "Without a way to measure progress, it's impossible to determine if anything is actually being done." Frequently, individuals and organizations have no understanding of what's truly being measured, the value of the measurements, and what interactions are actually causing the measurements.

Bubble Down

Bubble down occurs when an organization or individual starts to focus on a level of change higher than the one it's actually working on. An organization may begin by espousing transformational change but actually work on design, incremental, or no change.

Individuals and organizations are undergoing significant and traumatic emotional events as a result of the bubble-down phenomenon. A common result is an inordinate amount of focus on profit in organizations and a lowering of the standard of living for those involved with tasks. Focusing on one level and performing at a lower level causes great confusion for those involved in the process and for those who are exposed to it. Understanding the relationships of interactions is the key to design or transformational changes, not actions that are taken.

Cognitive Dissonance

Cognitive dissonance is one of the results of the bubble-down model. Cognitive dissonance is the result of saying one thing and doing another. This not only occurs at the high level of transformation and design, but also occurs daily in incremental changes.

Those at the top of the organization focus on the visible vector and rarely need or desire to understand how implementation actually occurs. Unfortunately, these changes are usually delegated to the organizational sludge, which has little or no incentive to see them succeed. Therefore the implementation doesn't resemble what has been stated.

Cognitive dissonance frequently occurs when teaming, empowerment, and reengineering are introduced into organizations. It's rare that these types of changes are carried out with any resemblance to what's actually said to those involved.

At the individual level we run into cognitive dissonance daily. Advertisers promise all kinds of benefits for using their products. When we find that some of these benefits are not as great as we expected, we are disappointed or worse. When organizations do something other than what they have said they would do, they foster distrust.

Copying Others

Copying the success of others is a path to failure since their key factors and their interactions are unique to them. Taking the ideas of others, understanding them and adapting them into your own unique environment can produce significant benefits. While this may seem like an obvious statement, few understand it. Benchmarking and competitive analysis have become a common way of doing business. While imitation may be the most sincere form of flattery, it's not the most effective path to success. In fact, it's a certain path to failure.

Focusing on Only Part of the Process

Suboptimization occurs continuously. This pitfall also correlates with pitfall seven, bubble down. It's much easier to focus on only part of the equation and call it something else. Efficiency and effectiveness are frequently paired in some form of continuous improvement or total quality management program. Creativity and adaptivity through reengineering or system analysis is often considered design change and improves the chances of success. Context is rarely considered, although occasionally it's the basis for transformation and revolutionary changes.

All five areas and their interactions are the basis for individual and organizational success. Those striving to follow the path to success must integrate these five areas.

Attempting the Impossible

Too often, individuals and organizations ignore interactions of key factors that will preclude their success on given actions. Instead they charge ahead and when they fail they place the blame on someone else. Individuals and organizations in our society have lost much of their willingness to accept responsibilities for their own actions.

To be successful, individuals and organizations must understand what's possible within their context and not waste effort and resources attempting to accomplish things that aren't.

Lack of Focus

Some symptoms that accompany a lack of focus are false starts, overadjusting, starting over, focusing on past successes, and too many hands on the steering wheel. Many failures can be directly linked to a lack of focus. Individuals and organizations often find it easier to start something than to finish it. Many conglomerates of the recent past have been broken back into their component parts to enable them to have a consistent focus on their marketplaces.

It takes much effort to understand the key factors and their interactions. When they're understood, it's possible to maintain a specific focus. It's not appropriate to continuously change focus. The visible vector to be followed should address the issues of the longest meaningful time-event horizon. It should be reviewed on a regular basis and be the foundation for changes.

Lack of Will

Successful individuals generate a will to follow. They also have a great will to succeed and are willing to attempt the impossible at appropriate times. They're willing to fail to succeed later. They're willing to admit their errors and to accept accolades for their accomplishments.

Organizations must have the will to explore new directions. They must have the willingness to change what they deliver, how they deliver it, and how they're organized. The lack of will frequently is the result of the lack of focus and not understanding the organization's context. Many organizations begin a program and then it falls by the wayside. This can damage the employee base in ways that are very difficult to reverse. This type of damage prevents the success of future programs.

Lack of Ability to Withstand Adversity

Lack of ability to withstand adversity relates to the ability to have things turn out differently than anticipated. This result is perceived by the individual or organization to be adverse to their benefit. As previously stated, value has meaning only to individuals. That value has positive or negative perceptions. It's difficult to overcome the negative perceptions when adversity strikes.

"You think you understand the situation, but what you don't understand is that the situation has changed."
—Putnam Investment advertisement

Individuals and organizations don't willingly kill their cash cow and transform themselves. It takes thorough understanding of the appropriate vector and their interactions to their critical factors to be able to accept the negative results of taking a significant risk.

FIFTY THINGS THAT WILL KILL CHANGE

It's difficult to develop a culture where change isn't just accepted, but it's expected. These types of organizations always have the "welcome mat" out for any new creative idea. They seem to always have a jumpstart on everyone else. The journey from resisting change to embracing change is long and can have many detours along the way. The following is a list of fifty things that will kill the organization's transformation from a change-resistant culture to a change-embracing culture:

- Not involving upper management
- Holding back from telling the people who are affected until they have to be told
- Expecting people not to resist change
- Expecting people not to be emotional about change
- Labeling people who choose not to change as uncooperative
- Selling the change to top management only
- Not requiring management to change
- Not requiring management to be role models
- Thinking people will be motivated by mission statements
- Letting the rumor mill be the primary way change is communicated
- Surprising people with the changes
- Not considering what other changes are going on
- Not worrying about the details, thinking they'll take care of themselves
- Not spending money to train the people who will be affected by the change
- Expecting people to change without changing the reward system
- Not addressing the stress that change puts on the organization
- Not considering the three leader groups—management, union, and informal leaders
- Thinking you can always make more changes
- Thinking the change team has all the answers
- Not acting on the ideas expressed by the affected people
- Misjudging the time required to change (too little or too much)
- Thinking there's only one right way
- Not listening to input from others
- Overemphasizing the good and underemphasizing the bad
- Misleading the people
- Not thinking that the success or failure of past changes affects people's attitudes
- Punishing risk-taking

> **"You can't truly manage change, because change is going to happen. What you can do is manage people's transitions through the change, how they think about it, how they react to it."**
> **—Lance Dublin**
> **President and CEO,**
> **Lance Dublin Consulting**

- Not treating failures as a learning experience
- Prejudging people's capabilities
- Not having a change communication plan
- Thinking you need to tell people only once
- Not rewarding all members of the change team
- Setting up an "us" and "them" attitude
- Not building on the old culture
- Thinking the old way was no good
- Not giving credit to everyone involved
- Thinking the change will correct everything so that future changes won't be required
- Not being willing to deviate from the change plan
- Thinking that changing or losing jobs doesn't affect the individual
- Not realizing the impact that a broken-up team has on the team members
- Thinking management is the only opinion leader
- Thinking you can manipulate people
- Management changing only superficially
- Not involving the affected people in the change design
- Thinking that one-on-one communication isn't needed
- Not understanding the impact downsizing has on both the people who go and the people who stay
- Waiting for others to change first
- Thinking change is easy
- Thinking everything that you learned in school is still correct today
- Believing that the old times were better

> **"Too many changes flounder today because the company tries to change its employee's beliefs, values, and work schedules, rather than change people's everyday behavior on the job. Stress new ways of working in your organization, communicate with people frequently, and reinforce work expectations with the right kinds of policy and procedures."**
> **—Bill Trahant**
> **Partner, Coopers & Lybrand**

THE TEN COMMANDMENTS OF ORGANIZATIONAL CHANGE MANAGEMENT

Professor Reid defines the following ten organizational change management commandments:

- Analyze the organization and the need for change.
- Create a shared vision and common direction.
- Separate from the past.
- Create a sense of urgency.
- Support a strong leader role.
- Line up political sponsorship.
- Craft an implementation plan.

■ Develop enabling structures.

■ Communicate, involve people, and be honest.

■ Reinforce and institutionalize change.

OCM EXAMPLES

The following are two OCM examples supplied to us by C. Richard Welsh, national director at Ernst & Young. The first (and best) example uses outside consultants and the second uses people inside the organization.

Using Consultants

The CEO of the company in question had a very positive set of assumptions about information technology, seeing it as a way to increase operational efficiency, thereby lowering costs and gaining a competitive advantage. The MIS executive was a rare individual who understood both technology and business, was politically astute, and could communicate well.

By acting as change agents, these executives gave the company an unusually strong start. Nevertheless, they called in a consultant to guide them in making the change in an integrated way, paying attention to the related elements of business strategy, information technology, and personnel. The first task was to formulate a clear business strategy. Eight executive vice presidents were asked to clarify their visions for the future in written reports and group meetings. The individual formulations were combined into a strategy for the company. Now there was a clear direction.

The next task was to get some honest feedback about what the executives really thought and felt about information technology in general. The consultants tried to elicit their actual needs, so that those needs could be translated into technologies that could help them solve their problems. In the discussions that ensued, the group realized that the company's middle managers, 104 people, were strongly resistant to change.

The only way to deal with this problem was to confront it head on by listing all the considerations of these middle managers. For example, they didn't understand the culture of the information systems group, they were concerned about the costs of the new technology, and they thought they would be losing control by using PCs.

For the next six to eight months, the consultants led this group through a series of workshops and meetings that helped them change their culture dramatically. The first thing the consultants did was analyze the current business by helping managers describe what they did and how that fit with what others in the company were doing. This prepared them for the next step; identifying what information they needed to make decisions about the business.

The workshops and meetings revealed many things, among them a shocking amount of redundancy in the organization, to the tune of millions of dollars. During these discussions, many middle managers changed their views about what information really meant and how it could truly benefit them in their work. All levels of management became aware of the horrendous cost of continuing to do business in the old way and became convinced of the benefits of sharing certain resources and information.

The change management process took almost two years, and it was not easy. This is an ideal way to introduce new systems, because it involves the users in the earliest stage, even before the system is designed. And, although it is time-consuming, it is preferable to the old way of introducing systems, which all too often resulted in theoretically perfect systems that were never put into place because the human element was ignored.

Using Insiders

The company that used insiders hired a manager to establish an ongoing organization that was chartered with carrying out desired changes. The manager had a sufficient technical background to understand the new technology, and he also had managerial experience. He was at the same organizational level as the head of systems development and reported to the chief information officer, who reported to the president. A strong marketer, he had a clear vision of the possibilities of the new system and was adept at managing conflict. The staff of his organization consisted of thirty-five people.

The work began with an honest assessment of the skill level of the users, the culture of the organization, and its attitude toward technology. Senior management was involved in the planning and in the communication efforts. The latter were quite extensive, because the people who had to use the new technologies didn't believe in them at first. To make the changes work, these people had to be persuaded.

The group developed an elaborate, eight-hour traveling road show with videos, discussions, breakout sessions, and more. Its title was *Achieving the Vision Through Partnership*—meaning partnership between the systems department and the rest of the company. A strong believer in honest communication, the chief information officer admitted that the information systems department had had problems in the past, and that it had made mistakes. He asked for the cooperation of all of the parties involved, and he established some role models among them.

A great deal of change was accomplished. New systems were developed and the users of the systems were very much involved in the process. Relationships flourished. New hardware and productivity tools were installed and used throughout the organization. New methodologies introduced by pilot projects and intensive training were effectively deployed. The change team used all the above-mentioned change strategies: involvement, communication, role models, change agents, organization structure assessment, and training.

The major problem the change team encountered was the unrealistic expectations of management, who gave the entire process only twelve to eighteen months for completion. They expected an organizational turnaround and the implementation of numerous new technologies—results that were impossible to achieve within that time. Under pressure, people became frustrated, disillusioned, and resistant.

It's imperative that the change process be given sufficient time to be accomplished. Change affects people, and they don't embrace a new technology overnight. The story, however, has a happy ending. Because the only major flaw was the aggressiveness of the schedule, the organization has begun to enjoy the benefits it anticipated from the new technologies. Actually, though, the change took three or four years to complete.

SUMMARY

"It's not the strongest species that survives, or the most intelligent, but the most responsive to change."
—Charles Darwin

Let's summarize by reviewing some thoughts on change management from some "people in the know."

A 2001 Gartner Group conference report stated, "By 2005, enterprises which have consciously developed robust organizational change management competencies will realize a 70-percent greater capacity for rapid adaptation than competitors that have not. This is important because through 2005 only 35 percent of the global enterprises will demonstrate a consistent ability to think strategically, but act tactically in driving widespread organizational change."

Daryl R. Conner, co-author of *Project Change Management* (McGraw-Hill, 2000), states, "It is inadequate to manage just project cost, schedule, and quality. Without managing the project's social impact, most projects will fail to reach their full potential." *And you will not reach your full potential.*

In a 2002 report titled "We Rewired the Enterprise," IBM stated, "We came to realize that important organizational change also has to happen in a company's social structure—in how people understand what is expected of them, in how they are rewarded and managed, in the way that ideas are shared. In order to deliver on our value proposition, we had to change the very nature of work."

Lou Gerstner, former CEO of IBM, stated in *MIT Sloan Management Review* (September 1997), "Change isn't something you do by memos. You have got to involve people's bodies and souls if you want the change effort to work." Robert Kriegel stated, "You may think your organization is in the groove, but if you stay there, it can become a rut." As the rut becomes deeper and deeper, it can become your organization's grave. This is exactly what happens in organizations that drive their employees into future shock. It's time to stop working harder and start doing things differently. Too many organizations think that they're in second gear and have to be doing 100 miles per hour.

"The cartoons of Buck Rogers in the 1930s showed uniforms that turned out to be remarkably similar to what American astronauts wore when they actually landed on the moon. No one was greatly surprised by the success of the moon shot. The prediction of a moon voyage runs through history. But science fiction writer Isaac Asimov reminds us that not one of the writers had predicted the most remarkable thing about the event—that when it happened the whole world would be watching on television."
—Walter Wriston
Banker and author

In *A Survival Guide to the Stress of Organizational Change* (Pritchett Publishing Co., 1995), Price Pritchett wrote, "Employees complain of being burned out, used up, overloaded. Too many of us are just plain tired, overdosed on change, sick of ambiguity and uncertainty." To offset this, we need to approach organizational change with a very systematic, well-designed methodology, focusing on the three parts of the organizational change management process:

1. Define how the organization needs to change.
2. Define what the organization will do to change.
3. Manage the organizational change process.

Too many organizations focus only on part 2, ignoring parts 1 and 3.

"A project is a lot like a three-legged stool, whose legs are processes, technology, and people. The project is only as strong as its weakest leg."

—HJH

Change management applies not only to our organization, but it's a concept that can be applied to everything we do. The reality is that change within us starts before we're born and continues after we die. Why try to fight it while we are alive?

Today no organizations can afford to sit back and let change happen in a random fashion. If they do, they'll lose their competitive advantage. Organizational change management often increases return on investment by as much as 30 percent. No organization can afford to ignore the impact that today's dynamic environment has upon its people.

Tom Peters put it so well in his book *Thriving on Chaos* (Harper Paperback, 1988). He said, "We must simply learn to love change as much as we have hated it in the past."

Summary of Key Points

- Managing change requires a holistic approach.
- Change occurs when expectations are disrupted; this disruption affects one's sense of competence, comfort, confidence, and control.
- Assimilating change is the process that occurs when people adjust to disruption in their lives.
- Change can have three types of impact on people: macro, organizational, or micro.
- The combined effect that the acceleration of change produces is a highly turbulent work environment.

- "Future shock" occurs when people can no longer absorb change without displaying dysfunctional behavior.

- Increasing people's threshold for change and reducing the assimilation effort required to adapt to the change increases competitive advantage and value.

- OCM is a structured approach for managing change that should be integrated with all major change initiatives within organizations.

"Change is a law of life and those who look only to the past or present are certain to miss the future."
—**John F. Kennedy**

INDEX

A

advocate 78

agrarian age 2

Ahmed, Pervaiz K. 114

Amazon.com 5

American Society for Quality xxxii

Arcement, Billy 12

area activity analysis xxiv

Armand V. Feigenbaum 35

as-is state 49

assessment, business drivers' 19–23;
culture 16–17; customer satisfaction 16;
historical change management 17–19;
improvement needs 17; present-state
15–31

awards 115–116, 118, 119

B

Barker, Joel 25

Becker, Brian E. 63

behavior 1, 110; and successful
organizations 137; defining desired 29–
31; reinforcing desired 103–119

Bell, Alexander Graham 55

benchmarking 141

black holes, organizational 74

Blomgren, George 114

boundaries 127

brainstorming 35, 36, 38

Bridges, William 53

burning platform 59–60

business driver 33, 39; assessment 19–23;
definition of 19; vision statements for
24–27

business plan xxix

C

Calloway, Bertha 19

Case, Ken xxxiii

change 1–3; and stress 82–87; anticipated
state and 55–56; as process 49–51;
commitment to 54, 90–91; definition of
10, 50; definition of organizational 3–4,
6, 15–31; determining a major 52–53;
implementation of 76–77; macro-type
83, 85; micro-type 82, 85, 86; objectives
of 8–9; prerequisites for 60–61; present
state and 55–56; reason for 8; resistance
to 77–82, 99–101; us-type 82

change advocate 62, 68–69

change agent 64–66, 79, 88, 89, 145, 146;
definition of 62; training and evaluation
of 66–67

change history survey 18

change leader 9

change management 7, 9–10; activities
during 121–137; and communication
60–61; challenges to 134–136; key roles
in 61–69; methodology of 49–101;
pitfalls to success 139–144; plan 43–44,